Anne Treneer was ... remarkable Cornish... her childhood in Gorran, and the neighbouring parish of Caerhays, on Cornwall's south coast. She went to the village schools where her father was Headmaster and then to St. Austell County School. Trained as a teacher at Truro she taught at various schools throughout Cornwall. She was determined, however, to continue her own studies and to become a writer. She went to college in Liverpool and, as an advanced student, to Lady Margaret Hall, Oxford.

Her first book, a life of the explorer and Arabist, Charles M. Doughty, was published on completing her B.Litt at Oxford. She returned to teaching but this time at schools outside Cornwall; although her heart remained in the 'Two Parishes' of Gorran and Caerhays, to which she and her sister, Susan, returned whenever possible. She continued to write, contributing poems to *The Spectator* and *The New Statesman and Nation* and sparkling short stories and historical pieces to J. C. Trewin's famous *West Country Magazine*. She published a life of the Cornish scientist and inventor, Humphrey Davy, and in 1944 came her masterpiece, *School House in the Wind*, which was deservedly hailed by writers and critics from all parts of the compass. *Cornish Years* and a third volume of autobiography followed before her death in 1966.

THE CORNISH LIBRARY
NUMBER FOUR

School House in the Wind

ANNE TRENEER

ANTHONY
MOTT
LTD

LONDON

Published by Anthony Mott Limited 1982
50 Stile Hall Gardens, London W4 3BU

First published 1944 by
Jonathan Cape Ltd

ISBN 0 907746 03 9

Printed in Great Britain by
Richard Clay (The Chaucer Press) Ltd

CONTENTS

TO CORNWALL

Great rocky scroll, graved by the wind,
Cut by the bright blades of the sea.

IN THE WIND

He panted to escape but I
As he was winding thin
And narrowly was slipping by
Gasped and drew him in.
          —On Catching the Breath

GORRAN School, with a house for 'master' glued to it, stood strong and symmetrical, without beauty but not mean, triumphantly facing the wrong way. It might have looked south over the distant Gruda and the sea; but this advantage was forgone in favour of presenting a good face to the road. Master's room in school, the big room as we called it, caught the north wind while the closets at the back caught the sun. I have heard that Mr. Silvanus Trevail, the architect, who designed many Cornish schools, committed suicide in the end; but whether out of remorse for his cold frontages I do not know.

The site—on top of Menagwins Hill, near Four Turnings—had been chosen so that the school might serve the children from outlying hamlets and farms as well as the children from Gorran Church-town and Gorran Haven. It made a difference where a child came from. No one could have mistaken Rescassa for Boswinger, Treveor for Trega-varras, or Trevarrick for Highlanes or Penare; nor could the people in them have been mistaken for one another. Far in the distance one would begin to recognize some peculiarity of gait or outline, or some trick of manner. Even disabilities enriched the person. Johnny Mingo of Rescassa had a hook instead of a left hand; but it had acquired so much personality that it pretty nearly was Johnny Mingo. I should have shouted, 'Hullo, Johnny!' if I had met it out by itself; and anyone would have waved a hand in greeting to my father's walking stick or to Billy Lawry's bowler. The children were equally clear in person and trappings. 'See what a hand-some great patch I got on me trowsers, Mrs. 'Neer', said a tiny boy of Treveor one morning to my mother, 'can 'ee see the sewing?' Each little group of children had its own clannishness according as to whether it approached the school by Trevinick Lane, Boswinger Lane, Crooked Lane or Menagwins. As for Gorran Haven children they were like the Israelites of old—everybody else was a Gentile.

Some children came from very remote farms, and the parish itself, in Powder Hundred, in South Cornwall, was remote when I was a child. St. Austell, ten miles distant, was our market town; Mevagissey and Gorran Haven were our fishing ports; Falmouth our distant romantic seaport. My father had come to Gorran as a young widower with one little girl, Ellen, whom he had left to be brought up at Poplar Farm, his own old home. On leaving college he had made village school teaching a definite choice. He had always lived in the country—my grandparents were farmers—and he loved country life and was suited to it. As he was lame he could not farm; he was the first of his family to teach. Probably his lameness had thrown him in on himself more than was customary with Treneers. When he was five, he had had what was known in his day as a low fever; it had left him with a stiff knee, and with a painful awareness of feeling. He told me once that when he was walking on crutches he had heard a servant say, 'Poor little fellah! It would be a mercy if the Lord would take 'un'. Perhaps it was this memory which gave him an intense sympathy with the young and weak; a hatred not only of illness, but of any talk about illness; a quick impulse to reassure any person who felt not perfectly wanted; and a determination that his own children should not suffer from any physical disability. He was cranky about our clothes. Our skirts were attached to bodices so that the weight should come on our shoulders, and not drag on our waist muscles. My sister soon compromised with her muscles, but I was loyal to my shoulder-bones for years.

He married as his second wife Susan Nott, of Brookvale, Gorran Churchtown. My Gran'fer Nott, one of the Notts of Trevarrick, was something of a saint from all I have heard, but handsome with it. Granny Nott was a Searle; she was clever, with a biting tongue. But on both sides of the family all I know of my grandparents is from hearsay; I was the youngest child of six and my grandparents died before I was old enough to know them. My mother, too, was a youngest daughter. She had had various admirers before the new schoolmaster arrived to cut them all out and carry her off under Johnny H.'s very nose. On our bookshelves there was an elegant copy of Goldsmith's *Poems* and a green-backed *Pickwick Papers* inscribed to Sue with love from Johnny. Apparently she was a great tease both to Johnny and Joe. My father used to laugh and say he thought he'd better have her as no one else would put up with her saucy tongue; and she used to say she thought she'd better take him, poor soul, as he needed looking after, and did not know what was good for him. He did not like roast pork.

The two were married in Gorran Church by Mr. Sowel and, without a honeymoon, went straight up to the School House. It was lonely at first for my mother. Brookvale was an old cottage in the centre of the village; the School House was on the hill, alone and new. Even the furniture, though some of it had been bought at sales, was new to its place, not treasured and settled like Granny's furniture. But my mother was house proud. Miss Elizabeth Lawry said Sue's drawing-room was the prettiest in Gorran, and Miss Elizabeth was a person who knew what was fitting. Certainly the parlour, as we ourselves called it, was a delightful room even as I remember it in its shabbier days, its first glory dimmed by time and children. I can still see its olive green and gold wallpaper, its carpet in darker green and gold; its comfortable chairs; the shining wood of piano and table, its yellow lampshade, and the books and music everywhere. It was a small room but was lucky in having four long, narrow, sash windows, two looking towards the distant sea and two towards Churchtown with its handsome grey tower just visible. The best view was from the back bedroom window. We used to say that we could see the Manacles.

At first the house seemed big to my mother after Brookvale; and her only disappointment, she once told me, was that her best tea-set was not new, but bought at Hemmingway's sale by my father, who fell in love with it and bought it without consulting her. Her heart had been given to a new tea-set she had seen in a St. Austell shop. For this reason or some other she never really cherished her wedding set, though its delicate egg-shell whiteness and painted robins on sprays of bright holly would have appealed to her if it hadn't been 'Hemmingway's old trash.' Yet not one of the dozen pieces was missing when my father bought it, nor was there a crack in tea-pot, milk-jug or slop-basin. He would remind her of this when the 'birdie tea-set' as we called it began to be broken. A child would smash a saucer banging on it with a spoon; the dog would knock over a cup; Mrs. Tucker would crack the tea-pot through using dishwater too hot. But my mother was unperturbed. She had, until only a couple of broken-handled bread-and-butter dishes and a cracked tea-pot remained, a kind of grudge against that tea-set.

She also disliked the exposed position of the house after the sheltered warmth of Brookvale with its orchard and gliding brook; its gay flower-beds and neat box borders; its moss-rose trees, lemon verbena and boy's-love flourishing among the vegetables and currant bushes. Granny Nott had been a famous gardener. But my father in his Gorran days had something of a Cornish farmer's impatience with gardening, and a good thing too, or the schoolhouse garden would have broken his heart. Except for snow-on-the-mountain, primroses and daffodils on the lower hedge in spring, and pinks, sweet williams and mignonette under the windows in summer, most of the so-called flower garden was in grass, bare and careless of the wind.

Except in thick mist or in high summer I hardly remember still air at Gorran. The wind either played or howled round our house; it rarely died altogether. It was a constant companion, in one's hair and in the leaves and in the telegraph poles, whirling the smoke down the chimneys, rattling the sash windows, and bringing the middle door to with a bang if front or back were suddenly opened. When I was told the story of Jacob wrestling with God I saw him struggling to open our heavy front door in the wind.

It was bare country; no trees sheltered the house. There were two stranded thorns at the foot of the garden, but they looked as though they had tried to run away and had been caught by the heels and retained the slanting attitude of those ready to race. Between the flower and vegetable gardens a long line of thorns had been planted and encouraged to grow as a fence. In some places these thorns were fairly high; in some low. We used to play the jumping game of 'higher and higher' over them, tearing our knickers, and scratching our legs, yet never feeling the scratches in the excitement. Jumping the thorns forwards and back was the recognized way of letting off steam if something really thrilling had happened to a person in the family.

The wind streamed round us straight from everywhere. From whatever direction it blew it met our house and swept on and round it like a sea-swirl over and around rocks. Winter gales were glorious. When the winds were really high, entering our house from the lanes was almost like getting into a beleaguered fortress. In the lanes we were protected by hedges. Then, tugging open our gate, we would advance a few yards in the shelter of the wall before running the gauntlet of the wind in the open garden. Sometimes we could only just manage to round the projecting corner of the house against which the wind would try to hurl us. It was called 'rounding the Cape of Good Hope'.

I played in the wind and my game was anything but elaborate. Sometimes the boys made kites, but I never aspired to a real kite. Any piece of paper tied to a string was good enough for me to go out and whirl about with. It was not with the paper and string but with the wind I played, hiding from him in a corner, encouraging him to pounce or fling or suck the breath out of my body.

The high wind was always 'he' and personal. I did not distinguish him by his different names in his quarters, but I soon knew his chancy nature, and could very early discriminate between the glorious South-West and the bitter East, though I could not have said so. The wind was associated with the Bible and Church. Going to Church every Sunday one soon knew the liturgy by heart, even creeds used rarely like the Athanasian Creed grew familiar. When the vicar said, 'The Father incomprehensible, the Son incomprehensible: and the Holy Ghost incomprehensible', I, proud of my ability to read the word, triumphantly joined in the assertion, 'And yet there are not three incomprehensibles nor three uncreated: but one incomprehensible and one uncreated.' When it came to 'proceeding' I knew it was the wind—'not made, nor created, nor begotten, but proceeding'. As I look back, Whitsun was a particularly lovely festival, not only because we wore our white dresses and summer was near, but because of the rushing mighty wind which preceded the cloven tongues as of fire. And I still think one of the best Old Testament stories is the story of Elijah angry with his God because he would not bend people to his will and make them conformably righteous. Elijah, like every reformer, had been very jealous for his Lord God of Hosts, and very anxious to liquidate everyone not ready to bow to Him. But when the Lord passed by Elijah, the Lord was not in the fire, nor in the rushing wind, but in the still small voice. When I first heard the story I knew nothing of the still small voice; but the rushing wind—yes. I was disappointed that God was not in the whirlwind. I suppose most people are. Only a handful of people in the world seem to know that God is not in the fire nor in the whirlwind but in the still small voice.

Gorran parish, though in South Cornwall, has a good deal in common with the north. It has the bareness and wide horizons of the north coast which is, after all, not very far distant. A giant could step from Dodman on to Hensbarrow and in another stride be over the Goss Moor and on to Pentire or St. Agnes Beacon. Cornwall is long and narrow. 'Nature', says Carew, 'has thrust it into the sea and besieged it with ocean.' Part of the enchantment of Cornwall is the bareness. Our Dodman shares this with Bodmin Moor, North Cliffs, Goonhilly, and West Penwith. T. E. Lawrence wrote of Arabia that its bareness made green fertility seem vulgar; in the desert he was drawn out of himself and held by the vacancy, by the abstraction, and by the weakness of earth's life in comparison with the greatness of the sky. His desire to avoid what he called his sultry self was gratified, just as for many people it is gratified, in a less degree, by the naked carns of West Penwith, the country of far distances which lies between Zennor and Land's End. Parts of Gorran shared this bareness; and its heady air, too, made it easy to understand what both Doughty and Lawrence felt in the desert. Those who have walked by Trevinick through Penare, and come out on to the top of Dodman, and looked into the sparkling intoxicating space, know what Lawrence felt when he reached the last crest and could look out on the Guweira plains. Somebody told me last year that he once met my father on the Gruda and my father said, 'I've come out to drink a cupful of air, John'. We are creatures of air, so it is not strange that we are unable to live in buildings long without an irresistible craving for freshness; and it is not wonderful that people should love the very air of the place where they were born. The chief of the miseries of exile

(of the world's unbidden guests) must be the sense
of being cut off irretrievably from the kindred air
and earth; ghosts haunt no unfamiliar places. My
ghost will haunt Gorran; but I hope it won't moan
about the Churchyard, or snore like a white owl. I
should be loath to frighten anybody.

The School House and Highlanes were the
windiest spots in Gorran. A wag once named the
School House Gorran Lighthouse. The Churchtown,
at the foot of Menagwins Hill, was sheltered; but
Menagwins itself, where Will Richards had his forge,
Agnes her shop, and Cap'n Lelean his coal-store,
was pretty exposed. Will Richards was captain of
the Gorran cricket team, and my brothers' hero. We
had our coals from Cap'n Math; my eldest brother
once said Cap'n Math watered it to make it heavy, and
Will Lelean fought him for the aspersion and won.
Most of the older farm-houses were sheltered, though
Trelispan, Lamledra, Tregarten and Tregerrick
caught the wind. Cotna was deliciously situated;
so were Trewollock, Treveague, Penare, Tredinnick
Treveor and Polsue. Trevarrick was perhaps
the best of all, where the earliest snowdrops grew.
The Vicarage was well placed among trees, its richly
cultivated garden contrasting with our wild one.

The parish was not altogether unwooded, but on
the whole we merited the gibe that Cornwall has
not wood enough to make her own coffins. There
were trees at Tregavarras, along Old Vicarage

Lane, and in the Churchyard; Trevennen Wood and Scotland were within easy reach of us. They may not be in the parish though; I am not sure of the boundaries. Trevennen may be at least partly in Caerhays parish, and Scotland Wood in Mevagissey. Caerhays, Mevagissey and St. Ewe were our neighbouring parishes. Caerhays parish had no pub; a sad reflection on that sedater place. There were great clumps of trees in Caerhays Park and beautiful woods at the back of the castle. Otherwise, except for occasional oak, ash, thorn, or sycamore, and the curiously twisted elms which made in winter a delicate frieze against the sky by Bodrugan, there were few trees. Yet I connect Veryan with ash, Caerhays with sycamore, and Gorran with thorn. One oak between St. Ewe turning and Highlanes was always known as Oak Tree.

The high hedges which bordered the roads and divided the fields were shelters for beasts and men. In sudden scurries of driving rain we sought a 'lew'[1] hedge. Cattle, seeking the hedges in wet windy days, would stand, their hind-quarters in comparative comfort, looking with melancholy eyes over the fields. Except for the moor-like stretches round Dodman and the Greeb, all Gorran was field and hedge. At Hemmick the poppies and corn and a lovely blue flower—I think succory—grew to the cliff edge, so that the summer wind

---

[1] Lee.

could be heard in the waves on the one hand and in the wheat or oats or barley on the other. Thomas Hardy has described the winter voice of the wind in holly and oak and other woodland trees; to hear it rustle the ripe oats is the luxury of summer.

There were times when we almost saw the wind. Just too late we would turn and it had passed over the waving meadow grass, or swept the upstanding ears of wheat; or printed the catspaws on the sea. I have seen the wind in light snow or swirling sand being the life of it. Snow is rare in Gorran. I always wish I had been born early enough to know the great blizzard, when the snow was heaped as high as the hedges, and the whole parish, the whole Duchy I suppose, was smoothed white and the sea looked black. My brothers remember the blizzard. My eldest brother was at Granny Nott's; in fetching him my father was up to his waist in snow, and they only reached the shelter with difficulty. There was a weird strange light in the mornings when they woke, and the dog went half off his head.

No words have been found to relate exactly the mysterious relationship of our bodies with the air—a body breathing air in and out, and surrounded by air except where the soles of our feet touch the earth. 'And he breathed into his nostrils the breath of life' comes nearest. When we walk or run or dance only an inch or so of each foot in turn touches the earth, and that only for a second. It is more wonderful to walk or run than to fly in a machine. That is ordinary in comparison. A flier in a machine is not flying; he is sitting down on something. Whereas a runner with the wind is as near being off the earth as may be. A human being cannot be completely and utterly surrounded by any element and live. In the air some tiny part of him must touch the earth, even if it is only the tip of a ballet dancer's toe. In water he must keep his head out, or his mother, like the mother of Achilles, must hold him by the heel. The less he has to do, tortoise-like, with enveloping himself in mud and mire, the better for him. He might find himself buried and know no more. Not to know anything! To be dead! It is astonishing that the idea of life should not be a conception so miraculous that for men to deliberately cause the death of a fellow would be unthinkable. I suppose Cain discovered only by chance that his brother was vulnerable to death; his horror when he knew what he had done made him a renegade. But before Cain was born Eve had stretched out her hand to possess what her eye desired. Children should be taught that only if they carry nothing in their hands can they enjoy the wind and know life from death. Then when heaven's breath smells wooingly they may sit among the sea-pinks and feel it gently lifting their hair and touching their cheeks; or when a great wind is rushing they may lean back against it and blow with it half off the earth.

2

THE FAMILY

Come out, sun, and shine upon us, Ho!
Here's a boy and a baby in a wheelbarrow.

My brothers say they brought me up in the wheel-barrow, and that this accounts for certain bumps in my forehead and general scrappy appearance. When I was small they used to tell me that old Mrs. Tucker brought me one winter night in a potato sack and left me on the front step; and that I squalled so loud that my father said to my mother, 'For God's sake bring the little Devil in and see if she'll stop that noise'. So in I came and stayed. And Mrs. Tucker stayed too and used to stir up the boys' porridge in an iron saucepan with a wooden spoon singing the while in a cracked voice:

Ort thou weary, ort thou langueed,
Ort thou soor deestrest,
Come to me saith One, and coming
Be at rest.

Any one of my brothers meeting another after a long interval will end by a high-pitched quavering render-ing in Cornish of this immortal sample of 'Ancient and Modern'. They will tell, too, of the time when

Mrs. Tucker put large portions of both sugar and salt in their porridge; and how my mother, appealed to, made them eat it to uphold the old woman's authority. This instance used to be quoted by my brothers as an example of the discipline which prevailed in the family in their day, before my sister and I arrived and were spoilt.

Certainly I was spoilt, though I was not, like my sister, a greatly desired baby. Indeed I have a certain feeling in my bones against the advocates of birth control. In their more scientifically planned society I should never have been, and I should hate never to have been. My parents led off with four boys —Maurice, Howard, Stanley and Wilfrid. My brothers, not liking their names, refer to this as mother's romantic period. A girl was greatly desired and when at last she came, and was christened by the good family name of Susan, my parents cherished her, but decided that they now had their quiver full. They sold the pram and gave away the christening robe. So it was that when I came I had to be wheeled in the wheelbarrow and be christened in nothing much at all. I yelled at the Font.

But for an undesired baby I snuggled my way in with remarkable ease, and I am convinced that there is no position in a family like the position of youngest, and no position for a family like the position of a schoolmaster's family in a Cornish village. Everybody knew us and made much of us. I was 'my lovely', 'my beautiful' and 'my handsome', though one of the plainest little girls ever freckled by the sun. Miss Mary and Miss Ada at the Barley Sheaf even used to call me their little jam tart; and Agnes at the shop, who had so ample a bosom that I firmly believed she folded up her nighty every morning and kept it there as on a shelf, used to give me 'nicies' and 'jaw-puller', a wonderful sticky stuff, striped pink, white and chocolate. Luckily my brothers thought me a joke and hauled me about with them as soon as I was big enough. So I was always out of doors. My parents had grown too used to children to be solemn over their up-bringing. My eldest brother says he came in for all that; and indeed I have heard my mother say that when Maurice was a baby she used to prepare his food while my father stood by reading the directions from a book. But by my time my parents no longer read directions from books, nor were nervous for the safety of their children. The others had grown and thrived, so presumably I should too if given plenty to eat and time to sleep, and space to grow, and training in telling the truth. This last training was so thorough that to this day I am verbally truthful unless given a few minutes to think.

Certainly there was plenty of space. Our nearest neighbour lived a field away. He complained that we tore down his hedges and trampled his grass. No doubt we did both. There was also plenty to eat.

Although my father's salary was small we had a big garden, kept a pig and fowls and bees, and lived carelessly lavish. I always thought we were rich. Indeed compared with most of our friends we were. Most of them were farm-labourers, fishermen, blacksmiths, or workers on the Caerhays estate, bringing up large self-respecting families on small earnings. Our farmer friends were richer but made little display. Old Billy L., one of the richest men in Gorran, went about looking like a tramp, with a green felt hat on his head, and his fiery little pig's eyes looking balefully at children out of his red face. John Charles Williams was as rich as a fairy tale. But he was Squire Williams. It never occurred to me that anyone else could live in a castle with a pond in front, and with a little house near the pond called (because Noah Loten milked the cows in it) Noah's Ark. We envied the ark more than the castle, and admired Noah more than John Charles. Noah was a genius with children; so was his daughter Nellie. Dear Noah! There was I suppose something childlike in his nature which made him free of the children's world. Other men would tease him. Once they took away the ladder when Noah was last man on a rick. Noah said, 'Now how be I going to get down?' And they said, 'Walk straight on, Noah, and you'll get down all right'. Noah in his dealings with children was the direct opposite of old Isaac in the village. Isaac walked with two sticks and would shout at children or fling a stick at them. Susan would run a mile away from him, but I, to show off, would pretend not to be afraid of Isaac. He would say, 'Anne, she idn afraid of Isaac, she idn'. He called my brother Stan 'old bumpy belly' because he stuck out in his jersey. This opprobrious term was joyfully seized on.

I cannot remember very far back into my child-hood. But when I look far back, farthest of all, it is summer, and I can see two great white wild roses growing in the sun in Crooked Lane. Every Sunday two or three of us, after church at Gorran, would go to Four Turnings, down Crooked Lane, and over the pathway field to Horse Pool. There we would wait until we heard the pony trotting along by Treveor, bringing my father in the trap from Caerhays where he went twice a Sunday to play the organ. If there were too many children meeting him to get into the trap we would run behind as a kind of wild cortège. When we got home the boys would unharness the pony and my father would throw me up into the air and catch me. In the trap I liked to ride in the back seat. I can remember when I had new patent-leather strap shoes, and was riding with Howard in the back seat. We had a dust rug over our knees and when we met anyone he would say, 'Stick out . . . shoes'. Then I would shoot my feet out from under the rug to show off the glory of my patent-leathers.

The back seat in our trap was safe enough. Not so all back seats. Once, years after the time about which I am now writing, my sister Susan had a funny adventure in Sam Kitto's trap. She was riding to St. Austell in her prettiest clothes, and enjoying the company of a neighbouring young man who was also riding to St. Austell in the back seat of Sam Kitto's trap. Suddenly the back seat slipped from its moorings and Susan and Jack were shot together into the road, while Sam went on driving hell for leather, and did not even miss his passengers for a few minutes. Sam's was a ramshackle conveyance tied together with bits of rope. Once Susan saw me off at Highlanes in Sam's trap and wrote to me after to say that when she saw us turn the corner and vanish from her eyes she felt yea even as Elisha when he saw Elijah whirled away in the fiery chariot. She thought she saw a mantle dropping through the air.

As a child I thought my father the most wonderful person in the world. Holding his hand I would go through fields with any number of fierce-looking horned creatures. But on winter nights we liked him to be out of the house. Though sweet-tempered he was sometimes moody, and he always hated noise. So our noisy games were kept for Wednesday nights when he drove to Caerhays to the choir practice taking one or other of us with him, but not more than one. We would take turns. He hated going

26

about with what he called a horde of children. When he was gone, especially if he took mother with him—leaving one of the boys or old Mrs. Dada in charge, we played hare and hounds round the dining-room, over the chairs, and under the table and over the couch. It was the most exciting game ever I played, and reached a pitch of noise which modern children would hardly dream of. My brother Wilfrid, known throughout the parish as Cap'n because he bossed all the boys' games, was a great brewer of wine—sloe wine and blackberry wine. He once made parsnip, but the stone jars in which he put it burst before it came to the drinking. My parents say that once when they got back from Caerhays all the boys were more or less drunk on a special brew of sloe wine which Cap'n had produced. They were too overcome to take the pony out of the shafts; but this orgy I do not remember. Apparently they bribed us with a glass of blackberry to go to bed before they began the real carousal.

When Maurice was away at school Mrs. Dada who cleaned the schools, or Carrie Spears, or Mrs. Clarke who did my mother's washing would come to stay with us while our parents went visiting. Mrs. Dada had a face like a map with wonderful wrinkles. It was she who provided the word 'niggybuggers' for the family. She told my mother one day that in the cold weather the wind blew so draughty up her open drawers that she had taken an old serge skirt and made it into what the boys do call a pair of niggybuggers. They were drawn in with elastic at the knee and kept the draught out proper. In the forefront of fashion, poor old Mrs. Dada! She would have been astonished to know that. But she always wore a skirt over them.

My father cared more for music than for anything else. We had a succession of organs and pianos. He was always changing instruments to my mother's annoyance. Once we had an organ in our small 'hall' and we could hardly slide down the banisters for the pipes. But at last my father settled down with a Brinsmead piano. It had a really lovely tone and still has—for he did no further swopping once he had got something really to his liking.

He hated teaching music. Sometimes he would be persuaded to give a boy or girl lessons, but unless there was some genuine talent he would soon throw it up and offend Mrs. So-and-so by saying that her son had the fingers of a sledge-hammer and no ear at all. He would not teach even his own children unless bullied into it. Howard and Susan were natural musicians and succeeded in making him set them on the way until they were old enough to go to St. Austell for lessons. The rest of us would start again and again, but give up in the face of discouragement. Of Howard my father was really proud. Howard played the piano as if he were a

wizard. At thirteen he became organist at St. Ewe
Church, a neighbouring parish. He was so excited
at this appointment that he jumped our row of
thorns up and down their whole length twice. He
could not play the pedals at first, but began having
organ lessons at St. Austell. Cap'n or Stan blew
for him.

In order to go to and fro to St. Ewe Church,
Howard was given the first bicycle which entered
the family. It was a Rudge Whitworth. Howard
went to St. Austell to fetch it and learnt to ride on
the way home; but he was so unsteady that when,
calling to mother to come out and see him, he rode
grandly into the garden, he fell off and tore his
trousers. Often in going to and from St. Ewe
Howard would ride the bicycle and Stan the pony.
They used to scorch down the slope between Oak-
tree and Highlanes. A Gorran Haven man told my
father about this speeding; the two were warned,
but continued to take the slope 'like a streak of
light', Dart at full gallop to keep pace with the
Rudge. One evening at twilight when machines and
ponies go fastest and my brothers were more like
a circus than usual, my father stepped out of a gateway and said, 'Stop, you boys'. The two had to
dismount and walk home, one leading the pony
and one pushing the bike. Moreover, the bike was
impounded, and put under the stairs for days. The
boys could do nothing but avenge themselves on the

informant, and the only part of him they found to
avenge themselves on was a pair of his trousers,
hung over his garden wall by the fuchsia bush to
dry. They cut off all the buttons. Nothing whatever could keep us from scorching. Later on I
used to stand on the 'step' of the Rudge, balancing
with my brother as we flew down the hills.

Howard was the best mimic I have ever met and,
as he played at St. Ewe until he went to College at
eighteen, we became familiar with St. Ewe person-
alities by hearsay and imitation. Mrs. Rasleigh, the
rector's wife, chiefly lived for me. She would be
afraid Howard would forget at what point in certain
psalms the second part of a double chant had to be
played twice in order that all should fit in and come
even before the Gloria. She was in the choir and
would turn round and bawl in his ear, 'So foolish
was I and ignorant'. Then there was Jimmy P.
the choir's main bass who would say of a certain
tune, 'Let's have un, I can do the bass of ee proper'.
My brother was inclined to play rather fast in
church, and was once furious because at a harvest
festival my father, who was standing by him, was so
irritated at the tempo of 'Come, ye thankful people,
come' that he beat time on the youthful organist's
shoulder.

Howard was nine years older than I, but he was
my brother of brothers. It was partly because he
did not go away to school as Maurice did, partly

because he was sufficiently older than I to find me amusing. My half-sister, Ellen, I remember only as a giver of gifts. She married when I was very young, and settled in Canada. Howard would do things for me. My father would take any of us who were ready out for a run before breakfast; but we had to be properly turned out, with hair brushed and shoes clean. It was hard to get long straight hair done when mother was busy with the breakfast. But Howard could be persuaded to take a hand with the brush, tie up my seaweedy hair, help me on with my shoes, and clean them on my feet in the wash-house, while I sat on the copper top. For this I would give him two great hugs and be off with my skipping rope or hoop down Trevinick Lane.

There can have been few people with more natural magic than my brother Howard. He had and has the vitality and gaiety that make all parties go. No one could be dull with him. 'Would I were with him, whether in heaven or in hell' people might have said of him as of Falstaff. He carried laughter about; there was no barrier between him and all humanity. When he and my eldest brother, Maurice, were grown up and home for holidays, I have heard people say in the same breath: 'Good evening, Mr. Treneer! Ullo, 'Oward!' He was ''Oward' to three parishes. Old Jimmy S. used to call him 'Owlard'. He has often laughed and said that porters will rush to carry a dispatch case for Maurice, but would see him (Howard) staggering along with a trunk on his back. His trousers get baggy; his collars ride up; his studs hide away; a back lock of hair sticks out, and a front lock stands up. He soon looks like a tramp. When we were young we made a disreputable looking pair together. Once when we were looking our worst we were in a field where was an upright granite block—not unlike a monolith, but put there within living memory for cattle to rub against. A pedantic-looking tourist brought up in the 'Hodge' tradition asked us about the block. Howard said in broad Cornish that it was called locally the Devil's Poker—it wasn't—and he made up wonderful tales about how it glowed red-hot on Midsummer night and the piskies danced round. When the person got out a note book and began to write it all down and said, 'That's most interesting, my man, I'm a collector of local yore. You seem intelligent', we were in ecstasies. He called me 'little woman'. 'And what do you know about it, little woman?' I gasped out, 'I've zeed the piskies, I 'ave'. For this piece of fantasy Howard gave me a ha'porth of Barcelona balls.

He had a quick temper and would fling anything handy at anybody when he was in one. But he usually missed; his passion would be too great for his aim. Once, much later, he was beside himself with rage when he thought I had been nearly knocked off my bicycle by an early motorist. He

stood there in the road in a fury shaking his fist
and shouting, 'You might have killed my sister'.
The driver was a little drunk and had swayed somewhat in passing; but he had been nowhere near
killing me. I hadn't even come off my bicycle.

Howard knew all the funny Cornish stories
ancient and modern for miles round and would
father them on our friends, using their voices and
actions so that in the end we would half believe them.
Local preachers were often pegs for these stories.
Many local preachers were the best of men, good
in their lives, and with a kind of earnestness which
was better than learning. They knew the Bible in
and out and round, and some of them had the
Cornish gift of eloquence. Others had more desire
to preach than inspiration for it; some in giving
homely details when telling the Bible stories made
them sound funny. One in telling the story of the
Gadarene swine said, 'and then all they pigs, they
took to their heels, screeching, and went slap bang
over cliff. And 'twadn no good then for em to
cry, "Chug, Chug", and rattle the handle of the
bucket. They pigs never come home no more'.
And there was the Hell-fire sermon which Howard
fathered on a mild man we knew: 'You do know,
some of ee, the little brook down bottom Mr.
Richards's garden; well turn un into 'ell and
'twouldn' make no difference; and you do know
the little river goin' into Portluney, turn un into

33

'ell and 'twouldn' make no difference; and some of ee do know the great Fal because you been a little steamer trip to Truro; well turn un into 'ell and 'twouldn' make no difference; and some of ee have seen where the Fal do flow into the great Atlantic where go the ships and where is that Leviathan— well, turn un into 'ell and 'twould be like spittin' on a flat iron. . . . O my brethren, turn away from yer sins or 'ell will get ee.' I used to fancy Hell might get me when I'd thrown a stone at Susan or done some equally wicked thing.

My father reassured me. He was a Christian after the fashion of Charles Montague Doughty whose younger contemporary he was. He would, I think, like Doughty, have gone through fanatic Arabia proudly confessing himself a Christian while interpreting it in a manner which Mr. Holman of Treberrick, a fundamentalist, ascribed to anti-Christ. Father's nature was attuned to every form of beauty, and particularly to the words and music of the English Bible and Liturgy. He believed, too, that children should be brought up in the traditional faith, and he founded the teaching in his own school upon it. But Hell he rationalized. I do not remember how old I was when he explained to me the irrevocable nature of words and actions and how you could become so sorry for something rash you'd done that being in a fiery torment might stand for a picture of it. T. S. Eliot has made that solemnity a new theme of poetry. I think there can have been few more understanding persons with children than my father. I ceased to shudder at Hell, feeling that he knew better than any book, but I always had a qualm when we sang 'Lo, He comes with clouds descending', a terrific Advent hymn which I nevertheless enjoyed. It was magnificently frightening. I imagined the great summons of the Trumpets, the clouds, purple with red-gold edges rolling up as at a stormy sunset, God in the midst with all the souls crowding to be judged. Hopkins can make me tremble still in 'Spelt from Sibyl's Leaves'. When I was little I had a notion that, being one of the best runners for my age in Gorran, I should be able to give God the slip and run away until His wrath was past and He was restored to His sunny Self. I was an adept at evading immediate anger.

Anger in our family was furious and soon over. Stan, my third brother, was the gentlest person, yet the most dangerous to rouse. He and Howard were great friends and never fought. But Cap'n, my youngest brother, used to fight with Stan away from the house in a corner of the boys' playground, where my mother could not see. My father, if he saw, would let them fight it out. The only time I saw them fighting Cap'n was down and Stan was kneeling on him in a fury. I knew the story of Cain and Abel and thought that this was going to be death. I don't think I was ever so frightened in my life, certainly not in any air-raid, as at that personal anger. Yet I have no memory of how it all ended.

Stan was the best of my brothers to go bird-nesting with. He had an uncanny knowledge of how and where birds would build. The boys had a collection of birds' eggs which I inherited. We kept strictly to the rule of taking only one egg from a nest and of not returning to a nest or disturbing the hen-bird when she was sitting. We feared to make her 'forsake'. In Treveor hill I can once remember Stan showing me ten or so different nests just on the great stretch of hedge and tree in the elbow-crook of the hill. We called birds by their local names—wrens were wrannies, and so on. Stan once showed me a cuckoo in a hedge-sparrow's nest. He was a bulging bird with his breast fairly bursting out of the top of the nest, and he opened his beak and gaped for food. The hedge-sparrow fed her monstrous child. Our friend the roadman used to watch the hedge-sparrow feeding that cuckoo and say she was working her poor little guts out getting worms for a great bird who was none of hers. Once in particular, I can remember going down Treveor hill and seeing a hen thrush sitting on her eggs. We saw her speckled breast and bright eyes and she must have seen our huge forms and yet she never wavered from the nest. Birds first out of the shell are amazingly ugly. I was terribly disappointed when I first saw the fledglings of robins. To think that these frog-like creatures were the children of the handsome red-breasts! Once we had a robin's nest in the rafter of the closet at the side of a part of the garden which we called 'the three-cornered piece'. We kept the door shut when the eggs were hatched for fear the cat should get in and eat the birds. There was a square open space at the top of the door for ventilation, and one Sunday the robin not only taught the birds to fly but, when we weren't looking, taught them to fly out of that hole. One little bird the cat got, a cat called Tweed. And Stan solemnly boxed Tweed's ears and explained to her fully that she was not to do it again. But a cat can't really be hit, and Tweed didn't care a tinker's curse. She still took a devilish interest in birds.

Maurice began our collection of birds' eggs and the other boys continued it. The eggs were in a large shallow box. They rested in their different kinds in little compartments made of cardboard. The box had a glass cover. To have this box of eggs to play with was a treat when I was small. The boys rarely allowed it. Those delicate shells, blue, and blue-green, and cream, and ground-colour, plain or mottled, in their different shapes and sizes, from big gull and pheasant to small sparrow and tit gave me a thrill of pleasure. By the time the box of eggs was bequeathed to me and I could look at it as often as I liked I no longer desired it. We had an ostrich's egg which somebody had sent us from South Africa; but that never seemed to me a proper egg-shell. It was thick. I saw a gull's egg bare on a rock, and the little gull pecking his way out of it. A woman at Llansallos once told me an amusing story of an egg. It was when I was grown up and was having a cycling holiday. I had bed and breakfast at a cottage where they kept cocks and hens and chickens. We were looking at them and my hostess, who was a cockney settled in Cornwall, said, 'Do you see that one with the red rag round his leg? That's our little Totty'. I asked why that one was special—it looked to me a scrubby bird. She said, 'She wouldn't come out of the egg, and the old hen left her. But we could feel life in the egg, so we put her in the hot ashes and she wouldn't come out. So we took her to bed with us, and I had her and she wouldn't come out and my husband had her and at last she came out, not out of the top where we'd peeled a bit of shell, but out of the back door as it were, and she looked beautiful, like a lovely little girl. . . .'

Wilfrid, or Cap'n, was the brother nearest me in age. There was only four years between us but, although we did some things together, we were never on terms of equality. He patronized me. He could do everything so much better than I, and he cared more for the ordinary things country boys rejoice in than my elder brothers. He had a passion for fishing, and it was he who best enjoyed rabbiting

with my father. He looked after the ferrets. He
was one of the best cricketers of the boys in the
village and was always wanting us to come and
field. I always felt extremely elevated if invited by
Cap'n to do something with him alone. Sometimes
we played truant for a day together. Once in particular we took a basket to pick blackberries so as
to propitiate the powers when we got home at night.
It was always easy to purloin something from the
pantry when we were making a day of it. It must
have been September, a hot close day, with a Cornish
sea-mist, and spiders' webs on the furze bushes.
We wandered and played, and ate blackberries, and
picked others for our basket, going ever farther
afield to find 'toppers' to make our peace-offering
more luscious and desirable. I know we reached
Dodman, for I remember the arms of Dodman
Cross coming out of the mist. We could hear the
sea moving quietly below, but we could not see it,
and the gulls were in the mist. And then we saw
a wonderful sight. I suppose the sun was trying
to come out and that the rays were in some way
refracted by the mist. We saw a golden light, not
brilliant, but mellow and suffused, yet with a core
of concentrated splendour—a sheaf of gilding. It
was the dull yet glowing gold of gilded missals. I
have only once at any other time seen anything
comparable and that was off the North Cliffs near
Camborne when the sun was struggling to disperse

39

a similar mist. Yet the effulgence is not where the sun is. On Dodman Point, on that day of my childhood, I thought the splendour was God. Cap'n was not sure that it wasn't. We stole home with no further eyes for 'toppers'. In Tewkesbury Abbey I have recently seen a disk with wooden rays, one of the emblems of the House of York which took as a symbol the sun in glory:

> Now is the winter of our discontent
> Made glorious summer by this sun of York.

In the old days I suppose the wooden sun was gilded and might have been a little like my sheaf of brightness. Mine was living gold, yet it was a glory made by the sun in another medium, not the sun himself in full shiningness.

From an early age Cap'n loved to shoot. He played with catapults and guns of all kinds. I was never a shot, nor a bowler, nor anything which acquired merit in Cap'n's eyes. I could not even make a flat stone hop over the sea (we called this game ducks-and-drakes) whereas Cap'n could make a flat stone skim and skip up to thirteen times or so. The only shot I ever made was an unlucky one. Cap'n for a treat had made me an elder gun. I've forgotten quite how it was made. It involved hollowing out the pith of a piece of elder and begging from mother a stay-bone for a trigger. We used acorns or aglets (haws) for ammunition. Cap'n and

I were seated on the garden wall, our legs dangling. We were fully armed, playing bandits. Along came a cyclist—nobody we knew—a rare occurrence in itself. 'Shoot!' shouted Cap'n. I shot wildly, and by some unlucky chance hit the cyclist in the ear. He got off and slanged us in good set terms. He said he was going on to Mevagissey and should send the policeman to carry us off to prison. Cap'n replied that he didn't care a cuss for any Pucky. (There had once been a policeman at Mevagissey called Pucky, so we called them all Puckies.) He shouted that we had a dog licence, and a gun licence, and nobody could do anything to us. I greatly admired the intrepid Cap'n for bringing in the dog and the gun.

We did a good deal of apple stealing. Once Stan was up one of the Trevesan trees and heard Billy Whetter muttering underneath: 'They damn boys been after my stubbets again.' But Billy was short sighted, and Stan was able to get away with full pockets a few minutes after Billy had passed. Our ethics in this matter were strange. We should never have dreamt of taking an orange from Agnes's shop, but apples were different. When I was about ten and we had left Gorran and were living at Caerhays, a girl called Alice decided with me to have a little store-place in the hollow of a tree for stolen apples. We would steal a nice lot at a time so as to reduce the chances of detection. But a boy called George found our store and stole all our apples. This act we thought most heinous, never considering that we had stolen first. My greed for apples once brought me to ignominy. The same Alice and I had been getting apples to eat in school. We had put them up our knicker-legs held in by elastic. But alas my elastic had grown weak with age and washing. As I went from my desk to get a book from the cupboard the elastic broke and plunk, plunk, plunk went my apples on the floor and were all confiscated.

My sister Susan was not despised by Cap'n because she never entered into competition. She quite firmly didn't like boys' games and said so. Whereas —apart from ratting and rabbit-shooting which I loathed—I longed to do all the things Cap'n did and to do them as well as he. When we added a special petition to our prayers mine was to shy straight, Susan's for curly hair. Not but that I should have liked curly hair too, but one shouldn't pray for too much, and to shy straight was the more important in my eyes. Nothing came of our petitions, but I cannot remember that our faith was shaken. We said our prayers night and morning as a matter of course, just as we went to church.

Our hair was a trial to us both—straggly, fine and long—Susan's almost fair; mine almost dark; but intractable, inclined to tangle, and requiring from our mother a great deal of brushing before it went into its nightly pig-tail.

Susan liked pretty clothes and wore them with an air. Clothes sent by our better-off aunts and adapted for the children looked better on her than on me. I was more at home in one of Cap'n's outgrown jerseys. Had shorts been in the fashion then for little girls I should have adored a pair, and I should have kept them up with a striped belt and snake fastener like Cap'n's; but we wore kilts with our jerseys, kilts which buttoned on to white calico bodices, clean on Mondays. On Sunday we wore 'best' dresses. Occasionally we had really new clothes made either by our mother or by dear Nellie Loten who was a dressmaker, and who would come to the house to sew. Our best dresses were sent us by London cousins. Once in winter we had little red suits with which we were delighted. They were miniature grown up suits—tiny tailored coats and skirts in which we both felt extremely dashing. We liked, too, green dresses made by my mother, trimmed with white fur. These had green velvet Dutch bonnets to match and edged with the same fur. But the glory of the bonnets vanished in our eyes when we went to spend a day with a certain Dorothy Onslow who was a visitor at Caerhays Rectory. We wore our bonnets, but Dorothy Onslow, a young woman of the world though only about Susan's age, laughed at them. I did not mind much, but Susan was stricken. She cried when she had to wear her bonnet again next Sunday. It was her turn to go to Caerhays Church, and she thought this Dorothy would be there to despise anew the out-moded and childish nature of her headgear.

Susan and Maurice were particular friends, just as Howard and I were. I did not get really to know and love my eldest brother until later when he was home for the long vacations from London. He was very proud of Susan and liked her to look nice. Once when he was at home for a holiday he took Susan with him to Mevagissey. In Farren's window there was a hat (a straw hat trimmed with a wreath of daisies) with which she fell in love. Maurice bought it for her and she came home proudly wearing it. Mother thought it not in very good taste but we considered it a hat of hats. Hats were not in my line and I pretended valiantly that I wouldn't have had a fellow to it if I could. But secretly I felt a pang or two of envy of Susan and her daisied vanity. Susan didn't in the least mind being thought vain. She laughed. But I liked to be thought a fellow who didn't care a button for clothes and, once I was out racing by field and cliff, or being a cowboy, it is true that I did not. But there were times when I looked at myself in the glass and wished that I had a less funny face; and it is said that I once cut off a lock of my front hair in a vain attempt at beautifying myself with a fringe.

My mother's hair was more beautiful than either of her little girls'. It was fine and straight like ours, but a rich dark brown and wonderfully abundant. As a rule she did it in a knot at the back of her neck, but was sometimes persuaded to make a queenly job of 'doing it on top'. Sometimes she would come into our room on Sunday mornings when she was dressing for early service with her hair down. It would just be out of its plait, long and wavy. We used to say, 'Go out with it like that, darling, it looks lovely like that. Don't put it up. Mr. Sowel will like to see it like that'. And she would laugh and put it up with swift fingers, standing before our looking-glass while we bounced up and down in bed.

It was the kind of hair which never went grey except a little on the temples, though she lived to be seventy-six. And she kept the clear colour in her cheeks. When we were children this colour was delightful, making her look years younger than other people's mothers. Her grey eyes sparkled when she laughed. Perhaps her ready wit kept her young, for she was quick at repartee. She must have been hard pressed sometimes with a family of six and a house to keep with no help except for the washing and scrubbing. She saw to the family finances too, my father not being good with money. I know from what she told me later that there were often anxious times when bills were pressing. Looking back I see that we should have been in an awkward situation if any of us had had a serious illness, and this possibility, I believe, often worried her. But this ill-luck never happened. We all had influenza badly once, my father in particular, but in general we were so healthy a set that I personally never spent a whole day in bed until I was grown up and then I only had measles. I cannot remember that any of the boys except Stan ever had to stay in bed either. Stan when he was about twelve had an abscess in his face. I can remember it though I was very small. He was taken to Mevagissey to Dr. Grier's surgery for it to be lanced, and when he came home with a great bandage round his face my father fainted. He could never bear the sight or thought of pain.

My mother was everybody's confidante. She had a deceptively sympathetic manner, and was a greatly loved person. Debonair is a word which would describe her for, although she listened to everybody's troubles, she could shake them more quickly out of mind than my father could. She was extraordinarily tolerant of human failings and, what is more rare, of human silliness. 'He couldn't help it', she would say; or, 'I suppose he was born like that'. She had, as though by nature and instinct, what the world chiefly lacks, the excellent gift of charity. She had by heart, 'Though I speak with the tongues of men and of angels', and saw to it that all her children had it by heart also. But her own charity came not in response to St. Paul's admonition, but by grace, as though by luck. She was no laborious Christian

46

or scholar, but a person with great natural gifts
whom life had softened rather than hardened. When
I think of her I remember Selden, 'No man is the
wiser for his learning . . . wit and wisdom are born
with a man.' She had wit and wisdom and she added
to these loving-kindness and an absence of hurry.
In a strenuous life she kept an air of leisure, the
secret of style.

3

DART

By the five-barred gate I hear him whinny,
Redder he is than the red plough-land;
But only his ghostly cob[1] I catch
With my ghostly hand.

I see him under a lew hedge,
Browner he is than the brown thorn;
But only a frisky shadow is munching
The shadowy corn.

Does he stop by muddy Rush-pool to drink,
Dredging it up through his lips so clever?
No! rushes and pool and pony and child
Have vanished for ever.

NEXT to the luck of being born in Gorran of likeable parents and of having brothers and sisters was the luck of having a pony. In the early days we had had a donkey—Jack—but I cannot remember him. He would go very fast when inclined, the boys said, but when disinclined nothing but a carrot would budge him. I never knew Jack, but I did know one or two donkeys—amongst them old Tommy Stratton's. Tommy Stratton came round the village at regular intervals with cotton and thread and tape-measures,

[1] Forelock.

needles, thimbles, hooks and eyes, elastic, and lace trimmings for underclothes. Tommy was a little grey man with a scraggy grey beard, not very wise in the head. Rescassa boys, in particular, would tease Tommy. There was a tale that once while Tommy was in a house displaying his wares, Percy Mingo took the donkey out of the shafts and then put him in backwards, and that Tommy came out and looked at this amazing sight, scratched his head and said, 'Now what be I going to do now!' I can remember a baby donkey in the parish, soft and furry, a perfect creature.

But our pony, Dart, was still more perfect. I loved him next to the family; indeed he was really included with my brothers and sister, though my mother did not think it reverent to put him in my prayers to be blessed with the others. I would 'think' him. 'God bless father and mother and all my brothers and sisters and Dart' was how I put it in my mind. Dart had his name partly from Dartmoor, he was a Dartmoor pony, and partly from his speed when young and flighty. He was small with a puzzled yet tricksy expression, and with a long mane and tail which distinguished him from other people's ponies most of whom were docked. But my father said a pony's tail was meant to be worn long to keep off the flies in summer, and that a mane kept him warm in winter. So Dart with long mane and flowing tail and a 'cob' over his forehead

49

by which we caught him and led him when he had no halter on was a kind of Samson among his fellows. When I was told the story of Samson whose strength was in his hair I saw him with a mane like Dart's. I used to plait Dart's mane for grand occasions and comb it until he looked as wild as a lion.

He was brown in colour and in winter his coat, unclipped, curled like a dog's. In summer the hair came out and he looked like a stable pony. He was kept in a field off Crooked Lane which my father rented for a small sum; later when we went to Caerhays Dart was kept on the Barns Hills above the cliffs between Pound and Portholland, a wild spot for him, though he seemed to enjoy it; he had a quarry to shelter in. I suppose having been brought up wild on the Moor he did not mind living wild when he grew up. He liked good oats though. I can see him now nuzzling his way into them and eating with a kind of surprised appreciation.

At first the boys rode bareback, but by the time I remember there was a saddle. This was bought one day in Mevagissey after Dart had suddenly insisted on stopping to drink at Rush Pool and had flung Howard into the water. First I rode bareback, but passed to the saddle when my legs were long enough. Nothing in later life can quite make up to a child naturally inclined to ride for not having the opportunity—nothing at all. It seems a pity that

country schools, since schools there must be, are
not provided with a few ponies instead of expensive
gymnasiums. Our pony could not have cost much;
we were poor. But what delight he gave us: more
than all the riches of the tin mines. He knew each of
us personally. Susan did not ride, so I was the only
girl he knew; but I fancied he liked me better than
the boys because I was so light. Galloping was the
fun. Galloping through the air with my knees
gripping Dart's sides I knew sheer bliss. There is
a kind of incorporation between child and pony, the
child's delight in movement mingling with the pony's
until they are more like one creature than two. Most
of my riding was after we went to live at Caerhays,
for by then my brothers were too grown-up for a
small pony. For riding purposes he became mine.
I would catch him on Barns Hills and ride over the
cliff top, jumping the gorse bushes. I think I hardly
knew then that the place was beautiful. I took it
for granted. But it was very lovely with blue, green
or slaty sea, black rocks, the rough road linking
Pound with Portholland, the white Coastguard Hut,
the cliffs leading to Dodman stretching out by the
sea on the left and on the right the cliffs above
West Portholland. Above the road were nine acres
of rough riding for Dart and me. We would
be together in all sorts of weather, rainy wind, or
bright clear sun, with a dance and sparkle in the air
which would make us both beside ourselves. No

later sensation I have ever enjoyed has equalled riding Dart over the Barns Hills unless perhaps motor biking after I was grown up—motor biking to Cornwall from the Midlands. I would ride fast on a Velocette with the miles speeding underwheel. Platform after platform thundered by (as a child once wrote in a description of a railway journey), my eyes vaguely taking in the great tracts of changing English country till I came at last to Launceston gateway and so over Bodmin Moor and to my own place. Motor cycling and galloping give the maximum sensation of speed. I have had little journeys in aeroplanes but that does not compare in exhilarating hurtle. To swoop up hill on a motor bike is a literal kind of ecstasy because one feels caught out of the body and into the air; whereas in an aeroplane once in the air and moving levelly I felt almost sedate. It is true that I have never flown a 'plane and that makes a difference. I would not give a fig to ride pillion on a motor bike. But to ride or motor bike over Bodmin Moor in sun and shower when the Moor is spanned with successive rainbows! That is unforgettable. I have been over Bodmin Moor when the rainbows have been scarfed about me. I was moving so fast that the bows changed direction until I was a dancer with the world for stage and the rainbows for streamers.

But motor biking is cold transit. Wear what you will the cold will get in and catch you, whereas riding makes you warm and gay and bold. Both pony and bike sometimes threw me, particularly if I was showing off. Once at Caerhays I had been out to fetch Dart when Cap'n was home with one of his friends. I came riding bareback down the hill below the Barton, and spotted the two walking homeward under the sycamores. I clapped my heels against Dart and made the signal agreed between us for galloping. We came tearing on, Dart entering, I am sure, into the fun of showing these boys what the Wild West could do. They turned as they heard the hoofs behind them, I passed them flying, exhibiting my cowboy ease, when Dart saw a piece of white paper in the ditch and jumped from one side of the road to the other. Off I came, my pride hurt far more than my body, for there were the boys laughing at me, and Dart, who always stood still when he had thrown anyone, looking with a mild demure sort of smile as though he couldn't jump over a straw. Except when in the saddle I was at the mercy of a very sudden jump sideways, having never had any proper instruction in riding. The only advice I remember came from Mr. Sargent. He would say, 'Heels down! Head up! Heart high!' Certainly my heart was high, but my head and heels were not unacquainted with the dust.

Dart was always something of a shyer even in a trap. But he should never have been put between shafts; he felt and looked far happier being ridden.

The trap took the life and grace out of him. It was, for one thing, too solid a trap for so small a pony, though quite pretty in itself with its dark blue wheels striped with gold. We never aspired to rubber bands on our wheels; ours were iron-banded. Some of our friends had rubber, and spanked along in silent elegance. Really for Dart we ought to have had something in the way of 'wheels'—two light wheels with a board between to sit on—which people used with donkeys. I used to admire just the right thing years after in Troon where there was an old woman who went with her donkey-wheels down to Camborne every day carrying hot pasties for the men's dinners. She would collect the pasties hot, and deliver them, I'm sure, not much cooler than when they came from the oven. For the donkey would go along at a terrific lick for a donkey. The old soul was known in Troon as the Galloping Major, and I believe it was she who said that if she lived and all was well she should be buried up Troon.

Dart could have gone more freely between wheels though I cannot quite imagine my father sitting on the 'board' like the Galloping Major. Ours was what was known as a proper turn-out. We even had trap lamps and a carriage umbrella. We needed both, for we were out in all weathers and often in the dark. Twice each Sunday my father, while we lived at Gorran, drove to Caerhays to the morning and evening services, and on Wednesday nights he went to choir practice. These were engagements which could not be cancelled by the weather. He would drive along the lanes by Treveor, down Treveor Hill to Penver Gate, and along Penver Gate to the lower lodge of the castle. This lodge was quite near Portluney beach. He then had permission to use the castle drive which cut off Portluney Hill, one of the steepest hills around. The drive wound through the valley. We did not drive all the way up to the church, but put the pony in the stable at the Hovel. This was a little clearing in the woods where there were two enchanting cottages—the head gamekeeper's and the head gardener's. There was a stable, too, and a shed for carriages. Into this our trap was put and the pony went into the stable to enjoy the Squire's oats and to worship as best he might. We walked through a level pathway field and up two steep pathway fields past the Rectory to the little church. When I glance back the sun is shining, the bells ringing, and the people are going to church in their best clothes saying, "Morning, Mr. Treneer, handsome morning'.

But one can choose a day to glance back into. Actually, though surely weather was much more seasonable then than now, there was as much wildness and wet as sunshine. And although in general the weather on that south coast is mild—with a great deal of mist and drizzle—it sometimes froze. Then Dart would go 'skittering' painfully on the ice in the ruts of the road; it crackled white. Once or twice we nearly upset. Coming up the steep nip from Hovel going home one winter night Dart refused to take the slippery road, and began backing sideways till we all but went over the bank. Straight rain we did not much mind, for we had a lined tarpaulin to go over our knees, and the great carriage umbrella over our heads. But in windy rain it was difficult to keep the umbrella up. If it were my turn to be my father's companion I would often drive while he held the umbrella over us with both hands. On winter nights in cloud the dark would be intense, the raindrops on the glass of the lamp would lessen the power of the light from the reflectors until the moving yellow cones hardly reached the hedges on either side. But going homewards there was no need to drive. Sometimes it was better to let the reins go slack and Dart would find his own way unerringly. He would arrive at our door steaming and curly; we would let the pools of water run off the tarpaulin, furl the umbrella with difficulty in the wildness of the night, and go into the warm parlour where the curtains were drawn and the lampshade cast a golden light, and the fire was leaping half way up the chimney. Being in is no real fun unless one has been out. Howard used to say as the wind howled round the house how wonderful the first man must have been who thought of making a great hollow space in the wind to shelter himself in; and I would feel unbelievably snug.

Longer drives were to St. Austell, our nearest railway station—pretty nearly ten miles—when we were at Gorran; or to Grampound Road, eight miles or so, when we were at Caerhays. We used to drive to St. Austell from Caerhays too, and occasionally to Truro, but this journey was very rare. It was too far for Dart. St. Austell was too far really. He would do it manfully, but he would turn his head into every farm lane for the first few miles, hoping we were going to see some friend or other. His last possible hope from Caerhays was Bosinver farm lane near St. Mewan. He would try to wheel into it; when that was passed he knew there was no hope for him until he reached the stable yard of the White Hart where we always put up.

After I was twelve or so and we had been living for some time at Caerhays I used to drive alone to St. Austell to meet one or other of the boys coming home for a holiday. We called them the 'boys' long after they had grown up and had begun, early, an incredible number of love affairs. I would be jealous of each successive girl brought home, but I would pretend not to be, and that I despised all this love. I denounced 'lovish' books. But I still remember the pang I felt when I met Howard on the station with Mary, his latest chosen and, I knew at sight, the real one. She stood there in elegant town clothes trimmed with fur—it was the Christmas holiday— and a white beaver hat over dark curly hair such as

Susan had prayed for. She seemed to have nothing in common with anyone as rough as I. I would not kiss her but shook hands stiffly and drove fast on the down-hills on the way home so as to try to frighten her. I would put my arm round Dart's neck on the cliffs and tell him he was more faithful than faithless brothers. It was I who had always been going to make Howard's pasties and keep house for him.

The best-remembered drives to St. Austell are summer ones when motors on our roads were still few. For years only Mr. Williams had cars. I would polish the harness and shine the buckles and clean the trap and groom Dart till his coat gleamed. Then I would set out on the leisurely drive. Sometimes until I reached Fair Cross I would not meet a thing in the narrow lanes, so narrow in some places that a tangle of meadowsweet and tufted vetch and loosestrife might brush against the wheels, and all would be a-dapple from the hedge trees over us. If I met a farm-cart or another horse and trap in the narrow lanes one or the other of us had to back into a gateway or into a bend in the hedge hollowed long ago for this purpose. Dart hated to be 'backed' and most people would back for me. Once a stranger would not back for Mr. Bellamy, our Rector, although he had the right of way. So he took out his pipe and *The Western Morning News* and began to read and smoke, declaring that personally he was in no hurry. In the end his opponent 'backed'.

After Fair Cross the Caerhays Road joined the Truro main road to St. Austell and became much more populous. We drove through Hewas Water, Sticker and St. Mewan; there was a fair amount of traffic even in those days and a good many tramps on the road. Susan used to hate to be on the road alone. After we had a bicycle between us, and she used to bicycle to St. Austell on Saturdays for music lessons, I used to ride the pony up to Fair Cross to meet her. She would ride her bicycle just ahead of Dart and me, and we would come frolicking along behind.

I remember only two accidents in pony traps, one in our own and one in my Uncle Dick's. In our own trap I was upset once when Cap'n was driving. We were coming back together from Portluney and had come Rescassa way—one could come back from Portluney by Rescassa, Treveor or Tregavarras. We were in the winding lane between Rescassa and Mount Pleasant, a little farm place, when Cap'n, going at full trot, drove too near a bulging piece of lower hedge. The step caught and we went clean over, pony, trap and all—Cap'n was quite dazed. The trap had been newly 'done up' and we thought we could hardly conceal the scratches. Dart wasn't hurt at all, luckily; nor were we.

The other accident was almost as far back as I can remember. My Uncle Dick was staying with us and he took my mother and me to St. Austell. His was a smart turn-out, a high-wheeled trap and showy-stepping grey cob. Whether my Uncle Dick had been at the Barley Sheaf or not I don't know—it was his favourite haunt, and there was nothing to prevent a man from driving when he had had a peg. We met a bus, a kind of wagonette with a couple of horses. Just as we were meeting it something flapped in the on-coming vehicle. Uncle Dick's pony shied and the wheel of our trap somehow seemed to mount the axle of the near bus wheel. We tilted in a peculiarly horrible manner; I can feel the tilt still. For a moment we seemed suspended sideways, and then I was flung with my mother out of the trap and against the hedge. The other horses were rearing and plunging. It was a terrific to-do until they were held. We were shaken, but not much hurt. On this occasion, however, one of the pony's knees was cut. The family story goes that my father's reaction on this occasion was not to be anxious about my mother and me but to say, 'Well, I'm glad it was Dick's own pony'.

We had other animals at Gorran besides Dart, but no one came near him for true companionship and the sharing of fun. We had various cats, but they tended to wander and to come back with paws hurt by traps, a sight that made me weep. There were three dogs—Floss, a spaniel bitch (span'l was the local word), Shot, and Nipper. Nipper was a fox terrier and my favourite. He would share a piece of bread and butter like a Christian, taking small bites in his turn. Shot was bad-tempered (a span'l like Floss) and we sold him to a farmer living some distance from St. Austell. He was taken to his new home in this farmer's cart, but in the night we heard him howling under our windows. Twice we tried to be quit of him, but he came back again, so we had to resign ourselves to him.

We had also cocks and hens and the pig, rabbits and ferrets and bees. Sometimes we had guinea-pigs, mice and bantams, too. We would put out bread and milk for hedgehogs. Cap'n kept the ferrets and saw to the little bells for their necks which tinkled and guided the gunsmen when the ferrets 'laid up'. The slinky, yellow, cruel-looking animals were not disliked by me until I saw a stoat kill a rabbit. Stoat and ferret seemed related—I expect they are—and I was prejudiced against the ferret tribe ever after. When I was first enraptured by Blake's magnificent cry, 'Everything that lives is holy', I still kept somewhere at the back of my mind the thought of that stoat. I could not be quite carried away by the splendid assertion.

4

DOWN BEACH

... Lift a nostril, and you get
The brown smell of a fishing net.

Lift an eyelid, fishermen
Are talking on the stick again,

Talking in their guernseys blue
Of what the government ought to do,

And would do if they had their say
Up the country London way. . . .

HALF our time was spent 'down beach'. I can see
the cracks in the sun-baked path leading to Hemmick. Cap'n said these cracks meant earthquakes
and that, if I stayed looking in, a big crack might
gape so wide open that I should fall through and
come out on the other side where my head would be
to earth and my feet waggling in the air. This horrid
picture would make me grasp his hand and trot along
at a good pace.

Hemmick was a mile or so from the School House.
We went up the lane to Four Turnings, up Treveor
lane to the iron gate, over the stile, and through the
fields to Trevesan farm. At Trevesan we often
picked up one or two of the Whetters, our friends;

then down we went through the remaining fields
either to Trevesan Bottoms or straight to Hemmick
Beach. A longer way round was by Boswinger Lane;
and a longer way still was by Penare. We usually
went through Trevesan fields. One or other of the
fields would be sown with wheat or oats or barley
growing high on either side of a path so narrow that
the barley whiskers would brush against our arms.
We would rub nearly ripe wheat ears in our hands,
blow away the chaff, and eat the sweet milky grains.
I have nowhere else smelt the hot August weather as
in Trevesan Bottoms. It was a mixture of bracken,
grass, bramble and honeysuckle steeped in sun. And
nowhere else have I seen such butterflies: blue, and
sulphur, and rarer orange-tips, brown bryonites, pea-
cocks and red admirals. They would wink their wings
at us. Dragon flies would skim with wonderful
gauze wings.

At the entrance to Hemmick was a little stream
such as runs into most Cornish coves. It had a little
wooden bridge over it, the water showing bright
and clear here and there, but almost choked with
watercress and great tangled growths of loosestrife,
comfrey, mullein, agrimony, mugwort and rushes.
We played with rushes, skinning them for the soft
white pitch of which we tried to make flowers. The
little stream with the rushes growing by it almost
lost itself as it ran down the beach and into the sea.
When I think of Hemmick of my childhood I think

of tide out and bare feet. I suppose we had clothes
to take off, but I don't remember them. The pebbles
were hot against our feet; dried crackly seaweed,
pixie purses and razor-bill shells pricked them.
Jutting from the cliffs were lightning-veined blue and
black slate rocks, with dolls' beaches in the angles
between them. Each little beach had its own shoal
of smooth pebble, its shells, its tangle of seaweed,
its driftwood, its sea-gulls' feathers. Feathers and
shells were our fortunes. There were shells with
hinges, and fluted shells; shells fan-shaped and
snail-shaped. Sometimes we found whelks and put
them to our ears to hear the ghostly waves whisper-
ing. Scallops we treasured to use as bread-and-
butter plates when we played tea-sets, or to make
patterns on our sandpies. The colours in the shells
were as clear as petal-colours: lemon, yellow, orange,
rich brown and a delicate mauve and pearl. Most we
rejoiced in shilly-billies as we called cowries. We
treasured them not only because they were rare but
because of their perfection, dove grey and white,
exquisitely curled in like wheat-grains. There were
more of these on Vault beach than on Hemmick.
Vault was a beach shaped like a bow which lay
between us and Gorran Haven.

Between the curving reefs of deposited treasure
was hot sand loose to the toes, and then the firm
sand, smooth or ribbed or wet, reflecting the sky,
over which we ran at full tilt into the water; or we

lurked in warm pools left in the hollows under the rocks, or we went with monkey hands and feet, toes and fingers curved like claws, up the ledges of blue rock spiked with limpets which ran down the beach on the right, and which separated Little Hemmick from Hemmick proper. I was half afraid of Little Hemmick. It was reached at low tide by an opening in the reef. When the tide came up it poured through this hole and cut off Little Hemmick except for the boys who could climb up the cliff where samphire grew. I never played alone in Little Hemmick. I was afraid the regular tide might play me an irregular trick, and the waves come feeling about their long sea-halls unexpectedly.

There was always something to play or do on Hemmick beach. We paddled or bathed off and on all day. I learnt to swim by what must have been a process of imitation, though I can remember the boys supporting me by keeping a hand under my chin. When we were not in the water we fished in the little pools, or went shrimping. Cap'n and Stan would go out to the farthest point to fish in deep water. Susan and I would make sand-castles and houses; we would design gardens set with shells and sherds and seaweed in order to play at visiting. Or we would go up the cliffs and sit on the soft tufts of sea-pinks, or on the trefoil we called boots-and-shoes; or we would pick ox-eye daisies to take home. There was a scent of rest-harrow.

When the boys had done fishing they would help to make a huge sand-castle fortified with stones and trenched round with deep trenches. We would then stand on it and hold the fort as the tide came in, a little froth first in the dikes, then lapping, lapping, until the dikes were down and the fort itself was attacked and washed away under us.

We must have eaten various foods on Hemmick beach, since we stayed there from morn till night. But the food I best remember is apple pasties. Each child had a whole apply pasty to himself with an initial cut into the pastry before it was baked. A for Anne, S for Susan, W for Wilfrid and so on. On either side of the initial a round piece of pastry was cut out, brown sugar and Cornish cream inserted, and the pieces of pastry put back. Sometimes we lifted these lids and licked the cream and sugar first, but the right way to eat a pasty was to hold it upright in both hands and begin at the top corner, biting on and on through mediocre and delicious alike to the last crumb of the bottom corner.

Years later I was amused to find that Celia Fiennes enjoyed a similar 'tart' when riding through St. Austell in the seventeenth century.[1] Her journeys were made in the reign of William and Mary and were first undertaken, she tells us, to regain her health by variety and change of air and exercise.

[1] *Through England on a Side-Saddle in the Time of William and Mary, being the Diary of Celia Fiennes,* ed. E. W. Griffiths.

As her bodily health improved she wished to occupy her mind, so she kept diaries of her travels, noting in them any information she gained from inns or from acquaintances and making, too, her own observations. She thought the keeping of these diaries would improve her mind and conversation, and she is earnest to persuade others, especially those of her own sex, to follow her example, and so rid themselves of the vapours. Moreover she ventures to think it would be good not only for ladies but for gentlemen to ride about England and describe it, increasing thus the glory and esteem of their country in men's minds and curing them of 'the evil itch of over-valuing foreign parts'. In the course of her rides she came to Plymouth and caught cold crossing by ferry into Cornwall. 'The sea and wind is always cold to be upon', as she remarks. It was at St. Austell that she had apple pasty. She writes: 'Thence I came over the heath to St. Austins which is a little market town where I lay, but their houses are like barnes up to the top of the house. Here was a very good dining-room and chamber within it and very neat country women. My landlady brought me one of the west country tarts—this was the first I met with though I had asked for them in many places in Somerset and Devonshire; it's an apple pie with custard all on the top, it's the most acceptable entertainment that could be made me. They scald their cream and milk in most parts of these countries

67

and so it's a sort of clouted cream as we call it, with a little sugar and so put on the top of the apple pie. I was much pleased with my supper tho' not with the custom of the country which is a universal smoking, both men, women and children have all their pipes of tobacco in their mouths and so sit round the fire smoking which was not delightful to me. . . .'

Celia suffered from smoke in Cornwall, sitting by turf fires, she said, till she smelt like bacon. But she is a grand companion to be with, undaunted by the rain driving fiercely on her. If one is longing for a taste of Cornwall and unable to get there one can do far worse than get up behind Celia Fiennes. She will soon show us things, from the little hardy horses, and the Cornish stiles, and the fires fed with turf or a great bush of furze, to the Mount, very fine in the broad day, with the sun shining on it. She had a heart for people too. At Truro her greatest pleasure was her landlady, 'an ordinary plain woman but she was understanding in the best things as most, . . . indeed I was much pleased and edified by her conversation and pitch of soul resignation to the will of God and thankfulness that God enabled and owned her therein, was an attainment few reach that have greater advantages of learning and knowing the mind of God'.

Sometimes on Hemmick beach we made a fire of drift-wood and scrowled[1] pilchards on a gridiron

[1] To toast on a gridiron over an open fire. Pilchards so cooked are called 'scrowlers'.

over the hot ashes. The sizzling pilchards of wonderful crispness and savour, though often scorched, were then placed on a great slice of bread and eaten as best one might. We must have looked a comic set of urchins seated round in a ring eating our pilchards. We were great hands at roasting potatoes in their jackets in wood ashes both on the beach and in garden bonfires. We cooked mushrooms, too, occasionally; but they usually came rather too late in the year for our outdoor feasts. By September, the best time in Cornwall for mushrooms, we were usually made to come home for the midday meal.

Occasionally there were big picnics arranged by grown-ups. Two or three families of people and children would converge on Hemmick, all with baskets and hampers, for food was the great thing on these occasions. Our games were better by ourselves, but for pies and pasties, cakes and honey, cream and jellies, the grown-ups were invaluable. No picnic was perfect without jelly or tipsy-cake. On one occasion, when we were having a picnic with various friends, Cap'n pointed to the spread—it was all set out on a tablecloth with stones placed on the corners to keep it down—and said, 'I'd like a piece of that swish roll, please'. We teased him about that swish roll for years afterwards. For in addition to the mispronunciation he had broken the rule that it was unseemly to display too great an interest in the food. 'Do not poke about the dish', as an old book of etiquette had it, 'the eye should, of itself, be sufficient to select the choicest morsel.' But certainly that roll was very swish with cream enhancing the raspberry jam in luscious layers.

People took immense trouble over children's treats in those days. The treats were rare; usually we were left entirely to our own devices, but when the grown-ups did take a hand they were generous. And, possibly because they did not too often assume responsibility for children's entertainment, they were wonderfully tolerant. They knew they could not get back into being children themselves again, but they held the ring as it were. Some grown-ups were always known by their Christian names; others never. Will Richards who kept the blacksmith's shop at Menagwins was always Will Richards, whereas the blacksmith at Treveor never went by his Christian name; his wife called him 'Jorey'. We said Miss Sowel and Miss Rosa to the grown-up vicarage daughters; and Miss Ada and Miss Mary to the grown-up daughters of the Barley Sheaf; and Miss Pearce and Miss Annie to the Tregerrick daughters; and Miss Martin to dear Alice Martin of High lanes. But how wonderfully good they all were to us! We seemed to be free of a village and yet private in ourselves.

Coming home from Hemmick after a day of end-less summer hours was a great toil. I remember the immense steepness of the first field leading up from

Hemmick, and myself hot and sticky with sand in my shoes. It looked as if one's short legs would never get to the top. We would go a little way and look back. Then at last one of the boys would give me a piggy-back, or two of them clasping wrists would make me a 'lady's chair'; or sometimes my father would come to meet us and carry me home riding on his shoulders. He would hold my legs one on either side of his neck and I would clasp his head.

Hemmick was our nearest beach, but the names of other near beaches, coves and havens also make music in my ears—Gorran Haven with Perhaver and Little Perhaver; Portluney; East and West Portholland; and Mevagissey in a class apart, for Mevagissey was a little town. My father went to Mevagissey at regular intervals to get his hair cut, and he would take a couple of children with him. Sometimes we caught Dart and went in the trap, but more often we walked. We walked past Menagwins and Penhall Gate, past the turning to Drowned Sheep's Lane, and came to a stile. This stile led through fields to Bodrugan Broad Lane and Bodrugan Hill. At the foot of Bodrugan Hill was Portmellon with a house or two springing up sheer from the rock, and another house or two in the valley. Sometimes it was impossible to cross by Portmellon; spring tide and storm would eat the road right up. From Portmellon we walked up and up until we crested Polkirt where the splendid panorama of harbour and coloured sea and coast was spread out before us. We would pause to look before going down Polkirt Hill into Mevagissey.

Mevagissey smelt. It was a compound of fish, cork, net, tar, seaweed and heady sea. The sea-gulls soared, swooped and screamed; they fought over fish; they swam with the water softly round their breasts; they walked on the quay (like gentlemen in tight boots as Dickens has it); they perched immobile as grey and white boolies[1] on rock or chimney or roof-ledge. The beautiful double harbour, the men in blue guernseys, the boats with coloured patched sails, the water green when the tide was high, the steps on bare, rain-washed rock, the ledges to walk dangerously on, the net-making, all the occupations of the harbour were a never-failing source of enchantment to us. We loitered and stared while my father was with Mr. Crowle, the barber. Then he would join us, for he, too, liked to idle on the quays, exchanging a word with the men as they cut up bait or dexterously examined and disentangled from ore-weed great piles of nets. These nets would be hung over the quay-walls to dry. Often the harbour was brown with nets, and the air was brown with the smell of them.

Mevagissey town almost seemed to hang. Its houses were ingeniously cornered together so that as many as possible were over the sea. Up the

[1] Big smooth stones.

containing sides of the narrow valley they mounted skyward or stood up from rocks by the quay-side. There were strange steep alleys, courts and crooked ways which would have been wonderful for hide-and-seek. But we did not play in Mevagissey. It was not our own place. There we were visitors and shy. All Mevagissey people seemed to live out of doors. Many houses were built over fish-cellars, up blue stone steps, and above these steps the women stood and talked in the open doorways. Doors were seldom shut in Mevagissey and no wonder; there was so much to see and hear and say. Who would stick indoors when the fishing fleet was putting out or coming in? Little towns ruled by the tides have an electric undercurrent; and yet an air of unchanging-ness and leisure and indifference to the stranger. No eyes so secret, under their apparent openness, as Mevagissey eyes. We were nothing; Gorran people, and bookish people at that, for ever excluded from the profoundest knowledge.

Even in Gorran Haven one felt something of the same exclusion. Gorran Churchtown was as different from Gorran Haven (Garnouan) as prose from poetry. Impossible to explain it, but Gorran was not secret; Gorran Haven was. My heart still turns over when I go into Gorran Haven. No little church moves me in the same degree as its Chapel of Ease dedicated to Saint Just; for no other church in Cornwall seems more saturated with the age-long life of a fishing haven. Yet when I was a child the church had not so very long since been restored to decent use; fish had been stored in it, my father said, and the men who congregated on the 'stick' were half hostile. But it stands there above the beach; within a stone's-throw of high tide, with the wind around it, stone, grey-slated and weathered amidst the stone and grey-slated weathered houses. It is like a French Cathedral in that houses crowd right up to the door; it is not isolated by Close or graveyard. Gorran Haven people must come to the Churchtown to be buried. 'Then at last he up and died', as a dear old friend said to me once at the conclusion of a long tale of a man's life, his marriages and bankruptcies and renewals of fortune. He died at the very nick of time to spite his relatives most.

To get to Gorran Haven we went by Menagwins, past Will Richards's forge and Agnes's shop, to a stile on the right. Then we went through fields to Gorran Haven hill. Near the foot of this the road branched and one could enter the haven either by Cooks or Rice. The narrow village street dropped nearly perpendicular to the beach. Houses flush with the road or up stone steps rose on either side. Here and there was a bush of fuchsia; or Pride of Fowey grew from a wall; or ivy-leafed geranium and wall-flower flourished where no soil seemed to be.

One side of the haven was protected by cliffs; the other had a quay running out, to make an arm in the crook of which deep still water slept at high tide. At low tide the sea went out nearly to the pier-head. Boats for fishing were dragged up the beach; nets were drying on the quay, and crab-pots and lobster-pots gave out their lobsterish and crabish odour. It was from Gorran Haven that we went out fishing in Johnny Hurrel's boat. Sometimes we sailed, but I never sailed a boat by myself, though I could row with one of the heavy oars pretty early in life. At one time we had yachting caps of which we were immensely proud. Wits greeted us with remarks equivalent to Medical Davy's when he met James Joyce in similar headgear: 'Where's she moored, Commander?' Gorran Haven children spent their lives in and out of boats, but they did not bathe much. They washed their feet as we called paddling, but not many of our friends except the big boys 'stript'. When we bathed at Gorran Haven we went in from Perhaver, but Hemmick was our main bathing beach.

Along the cliffs to the west of Gorran Haven the coast swerved inwards to make Vault—now I believe usually called Bow—beach. The cliff-path by which we reached Vault from Gorran Haven must be I think one of the most flowery in the world. Celandines, primroses and violets crowded in spring; not little starved primroses, but moon-like beauties with strong pink stalks on which the delicate silken hairs lay. In due season came other flowers, sea-pinks and horse-daisies and bladder campion and

75

honeysuckle. To stand between sea and sky with a floating scent of honeysuckle in the air, and the blossoms themselves 'revelling along in the wind' might tempt the gods to live in Gorran Haven.

Vault was not a sandy beach. The water runs like coloured light over shelly shingle through which the waves are sucked back in stormy weather with a wild music never rendered in words since the old English poets wrote the Storm Riddles and the sorrows of the Sea-Farer and the Wanderer. In Old English the rhythm washes through the consonants like the ground-swell through the shingle on Vault beach. Even in summer the sound of the waves below the Gruda was quite different from the sound on sandy Hemmick, or from the slap and gurgle by the quay-steps at Gorran Haven.

In soft sunny weather Vault kept its memory of storms stored in the flanks of Dodman which loomed up stark and terrible on the right. Dodman absorbs the blackness of winter in the same way as the sands at St. Ives soak up and reflect the yellow summer light. We called the Dodman, Deadman. Deadman and Vault; the names were permanent reminders of shipwreck and distress though we used them lightly and thoughtlessly enough. Yet something in Dodman subdued us. We never played there. Perhaps even through our gaiety there penetrated some notion of the irremediable dependence of man on elements beyond his control; we knew enough of danger to know we were not self-sufficient.

Adding to the solemnity of Dodman Point was a granite cross mounted on three steps. The lettering at the foot read: 'In the firm hope of the second coming of our Lord Jesus Christ and for the encouragement of those who strive to serve Him this cross is erected.' The arms of the cross stood out against the sky, a powerful symbol. We were awed by it. My brothers had known well the Rev. George Martin, a former Rector of Caerhays, who had had the cross set up on Dodman Point. I myself could remember picking up shells, a box full, for him to take to London when he left the secluded beauty of Caerhays to live, not as a Priest, but as a day-labourer in a London slum. He was one who took literally Christ's warning to the rich young ruler, 'Sell all that thou hast and give to the poor'. I have heard people say Mr. Martin was mad; my father thought him the sanest person he had ever met. To my parents he was a cherished friend; to my brothers at an impressionable age an unforgettable influence. I remember him rather as a hand to hold than distinctly as a person; he would walk in the garden accommodating his pace to mine. He would come to all kinds of meals with us, but especially to breakfast after spending sometimes the night on Dodman. He is the only guest not staying in the house I ever remember coming to breakfast. Chaucer's poor

parson had much in common with this remarkable
Christian teacher. Certainly it was true of him that:

> Christes lore and his apostles twelve
> He taught, but first he followed it himself.

On the other side of Dodman lay our beloved
Hemmick and, beyond that, the Greeb, a smaller
headland with great granite outcrops curiously disposed; a reminder of the days of the titans. Placid
sheep now grazed where ancient energies had worn
themselves out. The Greeb did not frighten us. We
climbed among the piles, and nestled into corners,
and ran over the springy turf. Except for a whitewashed coastguard hut there was no sign of human
habitation at the Greeb. It would have been a fitting
place for a hermit; perhaps it had its holy man in the
days when Roche Rock[1], a similar but far more
impressive pile some fifteen or so miles inland, had
its chapel and cell. There were no such remains at
the Greeb; but if I fancied an anchorite's life, on the
Greeb I would choose to live; though I should be
frightened of brother Deadman in the dark nights.
From the Greeb a coastguard path led over the wild
indented cliff-top to the next cove, Portluney. We
did not go to Portluney by the Greeb, that would
have been to go round the church to look for the
tower. We either walked by Tregavarras and down

[1] 'It standeth upon the wilde moares farr from common societie.'
—NORDEN.

through the Park, or we drove by Treveor or by Rescassa.

Portluney beach was a kind of adjunct to Caerhays Castle. I imagine the Squire must always have included Portluney in any bird's-eye consideration of his admirable domain when he was absent from it. The castle cannot be criticized by me as a building. To me it is like a poem or a face known so long that it cannot be judged. I only know it has an incomparable situation. Sheltered by rising woods at the back, it is set in a fold with Portluney as a shining jewel to grace the unfolding. Much of Cornwall is most itself in wildest storm. Caerhays Castle is loveliest in sunshine; it is civilized, almost Tennysonian, with gardens, and a drive, and woods where massed rhododendrons are at home, and azaleas and glorious white cherries. In spring there were sheets of pheasant's-eyes, narcissi and cultivated daffodils with princely trumpets. There were cyclamen under the cedar, and white violets.

In Trevennen woods, further back, wild daffodils grew. Trevennen is a smaller house which has not been lived in for years not, I think, since the days of the Dickersons; and Mrs. Dickerson was a myth when I was ten. I was told she had given me a doll which I was fond of, dressed in pink silk. Trevennen is as beautifully situated as the castle; to have allowed it to fall into dilapidation is bitter proof of the general stupidity of our time. What hideous buildings have been reared in Cornwall while that lovely one went to ruin for lack of use. When I have read novels telling the tale of strong men who have sold their lives for houses, concentrating all their force into a single passion for possession, I have thought of Trevennen.

At Trevennen, as at the Castle, Portluney is a distant beauty for the eye to rejoice in, the very sea taking its place as part of a pattern or scheme of decoration, disposed and controlled. While we lived at Gorran I did not know Portluney well, though at six I had been fished out by the heels from its biggest shrimping pool. But when we went to Caerhays to live Portluney, Port Bane (under the Barns Hills), Portholland and East Portholland became our nearest beaches. I grew to love Portluney then. I loved its clear brown river on the left, cutting off the most exciting part of the beach, where the caves and rocks were, from rare unenterprising strangers. The bladder seaweed popped under our feet as we scrambled about; long rows of waves broke on the beach—it was a wider bay than Hemmick. The only tamarisk trees in the neighbourhood, feathery tamarisk, grew on the hedge before the field leading to Portluney; sea holly grew among the bents in the dry sand above the tide-mark. Yet, as I look back, I see it all in an ordinary light, outside the enchantment of Hemmick. I had grown older.

5

FEASTS AND DIVERSIONS: UP THE YEAR

> Mary listened with pride and joy,
>   'Why 'tis a handsome little boy
>   Been born out here in the cattle shed',
> Shepherd after shepherd said.
>
> But when across that poor threshold
>   Kings came bearing gifts of gold,
>   Mary turned trembling to hear
> A soldier sharpening his spear.

OUR feasts and diversions depended on the weather and the Church, the two being intertwined: Winter with Christmas; Spring with Easter; Summer with Whitsuntide and Trinity; Autumn with St. Michael and All Angels and the Harvest Festival. There followed an interval for which there is no exact name on the calendar, and in which the Church celebrates All Saints and All Souls. Then the prelude to the birth again. 'Hark, a thrilling voice is sounding' was sung in church. Trevennen wood seemed to be waiting. Advent Sunday rather than January 1st is the beginning of the physical as of the Church's year.

I can remember when time was not measured at all; when it lay like an uncharted ocean about me.

In the midst of this immersion I can hear a joint conclave of boys' voices with a murmur from Susan: 'Christmas will soon be here'. This Christmas shone as something immanent and splendid. I suppose actually it is not that first sudden Christmas I can remember, but all the early Christmases at Gorran united in one chain. The boys would write my notes to Santa Claus and set them afire. If, after the paper had caught and flamed and dulled and shrivelled and turned grey it flew, light as a ghost, up the chimney, I should get what I wanted.

Mother made the Christmas puddings, with children round, tasting this and that, and all of us having a stir. There would be a wonderful smell of cooking and baking in the house, loaves of saffron cake full of lemon peel and currants, a great ham boiled and a tongue to go with it. The goose would have arrived from Tregerrick. For a week or two beforehand Christmas extras would appear in Agnes's shop to tempt our pennies from us, especially we invested in coloured baubles for the tree, silver trinkets and sugar animals. I remember in particular a pink sugar mouse which I bought, and a wonderful little bell which was Cap'n's and which tinkled on the tree. There was a silver star which went on the top each year, and each year we had tiny coloured candles in little candlesticks, altogether smaller and more fairy-like than the candles on trees nowadays.

The tree always came from Cotna. On Christmas
Eve we would take the wheelbarrow and be off to
Cotna where our friends the Kendals lived. We
brought home laurel and fir; box, bay and holly;
trails of ivy from tree trunks, and rich ivy berries.
Somebody carried the Christmas tree. It all seemed
festive, even Shot who went with us would be
spryer than usual and feel an extra stirring in his
tail. We decorated the whole of the downstairs of
the house; hung mistletoe over each doorway, and
then we set up the tree in the dining-room and hung
it with our treasures. The tree was never in the
parlour; that was kept fresh and clean for Christmas
Day. Christmas Eve was in the dining-room because,
before the lighting of the tree, would come supper,
for which even I stayed up.

A fire of wood and coal would be blazing, for we
had our own wood-pile at the back behind the traphouse, where we sawed up our own Christmas fire
with a cross-cut saw. I often sat on the tree trunk to
keep it steady on the 'horse'. The red curtains
would be drawn; the lamp lit; the table set. No
room cosier than ours on a winter night. The ham
and the tongue, as yet uncut, were placed before my
mother who always carved. She sat at the head of
the table; my father at the foot; I next him, Susan
next my mother; the boys two on either side of the
table between us. With anticipatory glee we watched
my mother make a preliminary incision into the ham

83

and cut the first slice, pink and white, thin and curling. There is no such ham nowadays; it was cured with sugar according to a recipe of Granny Nott's. The tongue matched it. We feasted. Apples and nuts followed and drinks. My father loved wine but could rarely afford it; as a rule he was content with a little barrel of beer on tap. But at Christmas time two bottles always arrived, a bottle of port for my father, and a bottle of something for my mother. My father had the temperament to be cherished by the grape. He should have had wine oftener. I can see him now, his blue eyes sparkling at the rare indulgence. We children had something home-made, blackberry or sloe. My mother's favourite drink was a little whisky or gin. She never cared for wine of any kind, whereas a stray bottle of claret or sherry would rejoice my father's blood.

After supper was over and the table cleared the great moment of Christmas arrived for me. We let the fire die down a little, put out the lamp, and lit the candles on the tree. I cannot account for the intense pleasure these tiny points of light gave me as they lit up the dark tree, the shining baubles, the silver star at the top, and Cap'n's little bell. There were no gifts. We did not tie presents to the tree nor place them at the foot. The tree was simply for beauty. We let the candles burn half way down and then snuffed them. The second lighting would be on Christmas night.

In the dining-room was a small organ. The lamp was now relit, and candles for my father to see the music. We gathered round and sang such things as, 'It came upon a midnight clear', 'Stars all bright are beaming', 'When the winter's sun was set', and 'There came three Ships'. My brothers had good voices; so had Susan and my mother. My father sang bass. I had an ear, and early knew the words and tunes so well that I have never forgotten them. But I had nothing to sing with. My notes like the house-martin's were inward.

After the singing, Susan and Cap'n and I went to bed to hang our stockings up. The elder boys sat up till later. But in what seemed to us the dead vast and middle of the night—actually, I am told it was late in the evening, before my parents had left the fireside—the carol singers came. Sometimes the ringers came, too, with handbells. My mother would come in with a candle to wake us. By its flickering light, sitting up in bed in the long-sleeved white nightdresses trimmed with embroidery which we wore both winter and summer, we would listen. I cannot describe the fascination of this music. The ringers would ring a carillon on the handbells and play a carol on them. Then the carol party would sing 'While shepherds watched their flocks by night', 'O come, all ye faithful', 'Angel hosts in bright array', 'Hark, the herald', and 'Christians awake'. Confused with sleep and with

85

the lovely story of the shepherds and the baby of which I never wearied, it seemed to me that everything was happening at that moment. The shepherds were on the Greeb, the baby was in a nest of Trevesan hay, and in our sky was the great light with the angels singing, 'Glory to God in the highest, and on earth peace, good will towards men'.

So far our stockings would still be hanging limp from the wooden foot of our bed, but magically when we woke in the morning they were bulging. Parcels too big to go into the stockings were ranged near; we would seize our booty and go into the boys' room. The stockings were all filled alike—nuts in the toe, then an orange, a packet of dates, a packet of broad figs, and a packet of sweets. The sweets were of mixed kinds, some noble, some common. With these we played swaps—a superior sweet being swapped for two or even three of a plebeian variety. The formula went: 'Swap, sir?' 'Yes, sir.' 'How many, sir?' 'Three, sir.' 'No, sir.' 'Two, sir?' 'Yes, sir'— or according to the bidding. This was a great game. The hazel nuts we cracked with our teeth; but pasty nuts (brazils) had to wait for the crackers, though I can remember Cap'n cracking his in the hinge of the door. The scene must have been of the wildest confusion. I would pop into Howard's bed, Susan into Maurice's, and we would undo our parcels. One of the best presents I remember was a picture book which on each page had a kind of thick paper pulley

86

at the bottom. One pulled this flap and the picture changed—A harvest field with corn-wagons and harvesters would become a Christmas scene with snowflakes falling on a woodcutter and his dog; three horses in a stall would change to a sow with piglets and a goose with goslings in a farmyard. There were more of these changing pictures. Another gift I especially remember is a humming top, and another a Noah's Ark with all kinds of animals. We would go out to show our parents the presents. I believed implicitly in Santa Claus when I was very little, but after a year or two the rumour reached even me that once upon a time Cap'n had heard my father drop a heavy copy of the *Arabian Nights* on his stockinged toe, and betray himself as all too human.

Christmas day was joyful, but not holy and enchanted as Christmas Eve was. We went to church in the morning—Maurice and Howard with my father to Caerhays, and the rest of us with my mother to Gorran. All the other children were in the choir, but I never attained to this honour. I sat with my mother about six rows back from the pulpit, and in sermon time snuggled against her sealskin jacket (an old sealskin bequeathed her by my richer Aunt Sarah). I sang my best and was proud of being able to find all the places in the prayer book. Hymn tunes carry with them extraordinarily strong powers of association. 'Sing ye the songs of praise' or Mrs.

Alexander's 'Once in royal David's city', with which Mr. Sowel began the Christmas Day service because it was a favourite with my mother, fills me with nostalgia; it brings back Gorran Church in every detail, to the ivy wound round the slender poles which supported the oil-lamps. We did not then know the loveliest of the medieval carols which later my brother Howard was to help to popularize. By the time that we sang at home—'The Holly and the Ivy'; 'Lully, lulla, Thou little tiny child'; 'Down in yon forest'; 'Green grow'th the holly'; 'As Joseph was a-walking'; 'The first good joy that Mary had'; 'Joseph dearest, Joseph mine'; 'Torches, torches, run with torches'—I was too old to feel quite that ecstatic pleasure I should have taken in them when I was six or seven. Some of the great hymns we had of course. My father would single out 'O come, all ye faithful', which, I can hear him saying, was magnificent; whereas he was scornful of Mr. Sowel's choice of carols. He would imitate the old parson's bass notes in 'Carol, sweetly carol', and say that 'Like silver lamps in a distant shrine' was nothing but tinsel. But I think I connected the silver lamps with our candles on the tree, and I loved them. I loved another equally despised Christmas hymn beginning 'Last night I laid me down to sleep'.

I cannot remember Christmas Day dinner nearly as vividly as I remember Christmas Eve supper.

I think when it came to the point I did not much like goose. In later years a couple of fowls were substituted for it; we never ran to turkey until I was nearly grown up. The pudding was chiefly valued by me because of the threepenny piece one might have with luck in one's helping. Otherwise I liked the almonds and raisins and sultanas and peel which were among its ingredients much better raw than cooked.

The best part of Christmas Day was the walk to Gruda with my father after the late midday dinner, and the coming in after it to tea in the parlour. Tea was in the parlour on Christmas Days. Commonly when my mother had tea in the parlour with a friend the children had it together in the kitchen— there were three doors, a passage and a room between. There is a story that once when mother was wielding her best silver teapot and enjoying Mrs. Kendal's company the door was suddenly burst open and a very dirty Cap'n appeared saying, 'Mother, Howard's got tart; why can't I have tart? I want tart.' But on Christmas Day we were all exalted to the best room for tea, and it was a tea after our heart's desire. We did not stay up to supper on Christmas night. Our parents must have been glad to get rid of us. After tea we played games and sang, and ate almonds and muscatels and roasted chestnuts. Then we went into the dark dining-room and, for the second time, lit the candles on our tree. But the glory had departed; it was never quite the same the second night. We let the candles burn right down, and the splendour of Christmas was over. Though the decorations remained up, and the tree was left standing till Twelfth Night, all had grown ordinary.

On our Christmas cards would be pictures of snow, robins and holly; but we never had actual snow for any Christmas I can remember as a small child. At Caerhays I can remember a snowy Christmas. At Gorran we longed for but did not get it. More often the weather was curiously mild. The birds of calm brooded over two little girls sitting up in bed in their nightdresses listening entranced to the celestial music.

Epiphany was a favourite Sunday with us. We sang 'We three kings of orient are' and 'There came three kings at the break of day'. It is a wonderful story, the story of the wise men who followed a star, and found a baby, and worshipped the God in Man. A cold coming they had of it according to Mr. Eliot; but to me whereas the shepherds were out in the freezing cold, blowing on their nails and stamping, the Kings came with warmth and colour and fragrance. I did not think they were ever cold.

After the Kings had gone with the various Sundays after Epiphany—we never relished 'Sundays after'—we began to think of the first primroses. Early snowdrops in Joe Nott's orchard at Trevarrick

were winter-white and cold, almost unearthly.
Lambstails and daisies, celandines and coltsfoot
would appear. Then someone would find the first
wild primrose. We did not count garden primroses
as genuine 'firsts'. Often the first would be discovered at Pitts, the cliffs beyond Perhaver; or in
Coosy Lane by Rescassa; or at Putt, between
Trevarrick and Trevennen wood; or at Sentries,
the steep fields behind Cotna, or in Polsue Lane;
or by Galowras Mill, about midway between Cotna
and Mevagissey. After the first primrose had been
found it was surprising how the families of buds
grew, and soon someone would bring in a tiny
bunch for my mother to wear; then in the twinkling
of an eye we would be 'going to pick primroses'.
We took a basket and a little wool to tie up the
bunches, and fairy-cakes to eat. These little cakes
made of flour, ground rice, sugar, milk and eggs
were as sacred to primrosing as apple pasties were
to sunshine holidays on Hemmick beach. We would
set out soon after midday dinner. Often it would
be cold in the early spring, and we would walk far
to gather very few flowers. We spotted the buds
and remembered to look for them the next week.
We picked half-opened darlings, and put in plenty
of crinkled leaves to swell our bunches, and feathers
of moss for a fairy edging. But when all the hosts
of the primroses were out we hardly knew which
to pick. I used to whisper to the glorious ones we

missed that it was not that they weren't beautiful. I had some vague idea that their feelings were hurt if they were left. Cap'n said this was very silly; that any primrose would rather stay in the hedge or wood. But Susan and I did not think so. We imagined that the other primroses in the family (belonging to one particular root) would think the chosen one exalted. We used to imagine the other primroses telling the buds what happened to some of their relations. Sometimes we put wild violets with our primrose bunches. At one place in Trevennen woods white wild violets grew, scented, and greatly prized. We hunted for the unusual and rare; double primroses, and red ones coloured like polyanthus, and branching primroses growing cowslip-wise from a thick central stalk. Now I think single flowers lovelier than double; they are more clear and delicate in shape. But I can still see in my mind's eye a wonderful double primrose my father once found. And the richly glowing double daffodils (we called them Lent lilies) which grew in orchards and in the steep field below Caerhays Rectory have to me the very essence and virtue of those who come before the swallow dares. The little single Lent lilies which grew in Trevennen wood did not dance; often they shivered. The double ones had dancing hearts.

All through Lent the primroses grew stronger and more fair and numerous. Even the earliest

Easter would find us with plenty to decorate the Church. I loved the season of Lent out of doors. The medieval poet exactly catches what we felt, though I did not know it then:

> Lenten is come with love to toune,
> With blosmen and with briddes roune,
> That al this blisse bryngeth,
> Dayes-eyes in this dales,
> Notes suete of nyhtegales;
> Uch foul song singeth.

We had no nightingales; the first nightingale I heard was in Shakespeare's country by Bearley Bushes. But we shared this sense of renewal and joy in the spring because, like the medieval poet, we experienced unmitigated the darkness of winter. There were only two out-door lights in Gorran and Caerhays parishes. These were the lamps over the church porches to guide the congregation along the path.

Lent, in church, I found fearfully gloomy. Shrove Tuesday was a good day, nearly always fine weather. But Shrove Tuesday was not celebrated in our house as it was in Gorran Haven. In Gorran Haven all the children ate limpets and winkles (we said rinkles) on Shrove Tuesday. But my mother drew the line at cooking rinkles or limpets. She hated the smell she said. Cap'n sometimes cooked some over a little fire out of doors in a treacle tin, and purloined a little vinegar, salt and pepper so that we should not be behind the rest of our world. But perhaps our mother's disapproval damped our ardour. Shrove Tuesday was not a great day with us once the pancakes were eaten. My mother did rise to pancakes.

Ash Wednesday promised well. It began something. My mother went to Early Service and we went to church at night. But 'Forty days and forty nights' was a very melancholy hymn. I was sad that Christ should be wandering in the wilderness and fasting. We went once a week to the little church at Gorran Haven in Lent. I liked this because of the walk down and back with Miss Mary of the Barley Sheaf or with my godmother, Miss Sowel. But once, alas, I disgraced myself. I was next my chosen friend, Phyllis Kendal. The vicar said, 'Let us pray'. I had heard it before a thousand times. But as we prepared to kneel Phyllis whispered in my ear, 'And so we will'. This for some reason I found exquisitely funny. I shook the kneeler with my suppressed mirth and throughout the service, when my mind went back to Phyllis's words, I was subject to relapse. The only hymn which broke the mournfulness of Lent was 'Christian, dost thou see them!'

> Christian, dost thou see them
> On the Holy ground,
> How the troops of Midian
> Prowl and prowl around?

94

Christian, up and smite them,
Counting gain but loss;
Smite them by the merit
Of the holy Cross.

We all particularly relished 'prowl and prowl'. We would prowl round the kitchen table in imitation and then swoop on a bun. It was grand, too, to be invited in the midst of the passive suffering of Lent to smite the foe. I did not know who the troops of Midian were, but certainly I up and smote them with such poor voice as I had.

Palm Sunday came with its brief success, the shouting and the glory. 'Ride on, ride on, in Majesty' was one of our very favourite hymns. 'All glory, laud and honour' was second to it. We followed the events of Holy Week to the Agony in the Garden, the Crucifixion, and the placing of the Body in the sealed tomb. A child is, I think, in some sort protected from the realization of the torture of the Crucifixion. It was not until I was grown up that the most profoundly moving words ever spoken: 'My God, my God, why hast Thou forsaken me' became truly significant in my mind. As a child it was the failure of the human relationship between St. Peter and Jesus which made me cry: 'And the Lord turned and looked upon Peter'. Peter is, I suppose, naturally a sympathetic character to a child; his desertion something which one longs to avert. Surely it will not be Peter who will say he never knew his friend.

As a child I never attended a three hours' service on Good Friday. On Good Friday afternoon we went to pick primroses for the Easter decorations, on Saturday we decorated, and then came Easter Sunday. One was supposed to wear something new on Easter Sunday, even if it were only a new hair-ribbon; otherwise a little bird would come and leave droppings on one's hat. I can remember my Aunt Eliza sending my mother a new hat for Easter Sunday so that this fate might be averted. We thought it a most becoming hat, and cheered my mother on to wear it; but she thought it too near the height of fashion. She didn't 'feel comfortable in it'. She loved old clothes, in this reversing the usual position between husband and wife. For my father liked a new spring suiting. The tradition at Gorran was that children should go without coats on Easter Sunday morning. There was dismay if my mother considered it too cold and refused permission to shed winter husks and show our frocks. We were sure other children's mothers would let them come without coats. And it is true that most of them did unless it actually rained. The physical warmth of childhood seemed inexhaustible. I hardly remember feeling cold. We hated coats and hats. As for gloves we never wore them except on Sundays. Elevated into wearing a pair of white cottons for Miss Rosa Sowel's wedding I am reported to have said loudly in church, 'Take off gloves, hands can't see'. There is a muffled blindness in wearing gloves, I still think. I dimly remember Miss Rosa's wedding, a great affair. Susan had a new white frock for it, and I had one of Susan's old ones hemmed up. It shows how self-centred we were. I can see our frocks but not Miss Rosa's; yet I loved Miss Rosa, who made me daisy and buttercup chains and played endless games with me on the Vicarage lawn. She would let me crawl under the net to pick and eat the old parson's red and white currants or raspberries. He would say, 'Oh, oh, oh, who is that white blackbird under my raspberry net!'

He was a very very old man with a long white beard, and a fussy staccato manner; very absent-minded. I did not like him much, for I never knew what he would do or say when I met him. From my present mature viewpoint I can see that he was facetious with children and that I, like all small children, was wounded in my dignity by this form of condescension. With my brothers he managed better. When well over eighty he got up at half past five in the morning to wish luck to my brother Stan who was going up to London for a civil service examination. Howard was driving the examinee in the trap to St. Austell station. As they were driving along Old Vicarage Lane they heard a voice shouting, 'Stop them, Billy, stop them'. Billy Tregilgas came panting through the plantation to intercept them, and behind him came the old parson with his beard in the wind to give his favourite his blessing. Stan passed his examination and was well up on the list too—although that trip to London was the first time he had been out of Cornwall, and he had been coached by no one but my father.

Easter Sunday morning was the old parson's great day. He looked magnificently pastoral. The sun would be shining and the birds singing outside the church. 'Jesus Christ is risen today', we sang. The glorious affirmation, the fine tune, the rising sap, and the jubilant birds—there was no doubt at all about it. Death and winter had been vanquished. 'The strife is o'er, the battle done; Alleluia!' There was another hymn I liked, but I have forgotten how it began. One verse of it was:

> And now the time of singing
> Is come for every bird;
> And over all the country
> The turtle dove is heard:
>
> The fig her green fruit ripens,
> The vines are in their bloom;
> Arise and smell their fragrance,
> My love, my fair one, come!

Best of all at Easter I think I liked and still like the story of Mary meeting Jesus in the garden. What other narrative approaches it?

'The first day of the week cometh Mary Magdalene early, when it was yet dark, unto the sepulchre, and seeth the stone taken away from the sepulchre. Then she runneth, and cometh to Simon Peter, and to the other disciple whom Jesus loved, and saith unto them, They have taken away the Lord out of the sepulchre, and we know not where they have laid him.

'Peter therefore went forth, and that other disciple, and came to the sepulchre. So they ran both together: and the other disciple did outrun Peter, and came first to the sepulchre. And he stooping down, and looking in, saw the linen clothes lying; yet went he not in.

'Then cometh Simon Peter following him, and went into the sepulchre, and seeth the linen clothes lie, and the napkin, that was about his head, not lying with the linen clothes, but wrapped together in a place by itself. Then went in also that other disciple which came first to the sepulchre, and he saw, and believed. For as yet they knew not the scripture, that he must rise again from the dead.

'Then the disciples went away again unto their own home.

'But Mary stood without at the sepulchre weeping: and as she wept, she stooped down, and looked into the sepulchre, and seeth two angels in white sitting, the one at the head, and the other at the feet, where the body of Jesus had lain.

'And they say unto her, Woman, why weepest thou? She saith unto them, Because they have taken away my Lord, and I know not where they have laid him. And when she had thus said, she turned herself back, and saw Jesus standing, and knew not that it was Jesus.

'Jesus saith unto her, Woman, why weepest thou? Whom seekest thou? She, supposing him to be the gardener, saith unto him, Sir, if thou have borne him hence, tell me where thou hast laid him, and I will take him away. Jesus saith unto her, Mary! She turned herself, and saith unto him, Rabboni! which is to say, Master!'

In the week after Easter came Gorran Feast. It sounded in anticipation better than it was. We would be running to the first gate in Menagwins Lane to look down on the village to see if the first 'standing' had come. In my brothers' young days Gorran Feast had been far more important than in mine; in my mother's day more important still. By the time I remember it, it had dwindled to about two or three standings. I remember Mrs. Hooper, a rosy cheeked, roundabout little woman, with grey hair in a bun. Her standing displayed long sticks of rock, huge oranges (oranges were at their sweetest at about Gorran Feast time), liquorice—we made liquorice-water and kept our bottles in the dark for a short spell because we thought the liquid went the blacker for it—gingerbreads, jaw-puller, comfits, dolly-day-dreams, mixed nuts, and all kinds of mixed sweets. These were grand material for the

game of 'Swap, sir!' Jimmy Ivy's standing is the
other I remember. It sold toys, and strings of beads,
and beads in boxes with glass tops, and toy watches.
I bought a toy watch for which I paid threepence;
but Cap'n took it to pieces to see how it was made.
Only one year did Gorran Feast really make an
impression on us and that was when the swing-boats
came. There were plenty of ordinary swings in
Gorran. We had a swing ourselves, and nearly all
our friends had swings in their gardens or barns.
But these swings were glorified beyond recognition.
I had my first swing with Howard. We sat opposite
one another and crossed ropes. These ropes looked
like the ropes of church bells and had the same red
hand-grips to keep the ropes from galling the hands.
Howard pulled gently at first; and I pulled back.
We swung. He pulled a little harder, I pulled a
little harder; we swung higher. Then we warmed
up to it as he saw I was not frightened. Up I went
like a bird, my head low and my feet pointing skyward; then down, down with the bottom seeming to
drop out of my world. Down, down, and then up,
my head high now and feet earthwards. Higher and
higher, the wind lifting my long hair as I flew. I
was beside myself with pleasure. When the show-
man ran the plank under us to stop the swing-boat I
did nothing but beg for more swings—I having spent
all my pennies on dolly-day-dreams (little sweets
much affected by Susan and me because we got so

many for the money) and a Jimmy Ivy watch. I
begged swings from my brothers and shamelessly
from others not my kin. I know dear Noah Loten
gave me a swing. I think never, except possibly
when I first heard Sammy Rowe's string band, had
I been so much excited as by those swing-boats.

Our own swing was hung from a tree at the
bottom of the garden. But after the swing-boats at
Gorran Feast we tried to fix up a kind of swing-boat
in the wash-house. Instead of cross-ropes and two
people in the boat, we had one person in the boat
pulling himself by a rope (with a blue sash wound
round for a hand-grip in imitation of the grandeur
of the swing-boat grips) fastened to a staple in the
wall. The boys despised this home-made boat once
they had contrived it, but Susan and I used it a
great deal until the craze died down. We had at the
same time a craze for what we called cork-work,
though it was done not with a cork but an empty
cotton reel. We would take a reel down to John
Parnel who had a cobbler's shop in a little wooden
house on the Plosh in Churchtown. John Parnel
made and mended our shoes; he was very obliging
and nice to children. He was a little bent old lame
man. He would put the sprigs in our reel. We
would then proceed to 'Ollie's'—Miss Olive Oliver's
shop—and buy ha'porths of wool of different gay
colours. Susan would then start the cork-work. I have
forgotten how we did it but it involved a hairpin.

We always meant to make a lamp mat of it for my mother, but never succeeded. The idea was that one of us would do a little cork-work while the other had a swing, and so on alternately. We timed it so that one had to bring a colour down through the reel before one could claim a swing. Although usually good-tempered with each other we nearly always ended in a furious quarrel over this game. We would accuse each other of not doing a fair amount of cork-work before claiming the swing-boat. In the end we would fight each other as like as not, not formally like the boys, but making for each other's hair to pull. Our anger was soon over though. However 'vexed', we could not do without each other for long; and after a fight and a separation we would soon be only too ready to 'make it up'. Soon, entwined on the old couch in the dining-room, we would forget the cork-work and the swing, and Susan would read my favourite Grimm's fairy tale, *Under the Juniper Tree* or *The Twelve Dancing Princesses*.

From Gorran Feast to Midsummer was a golden time. When the sap was rising Cap'n would make me a sycamore whistle. Sycamore was the only tree I noticed much, I suppose because of the beautiful colour of the buds and early shoots, pink and red and bronze, and the fan-like opening of the crinkled leaves. Sycamore and ferns; the curled hart's tongues with downy backs, the bracken on the Greeb which opened later. Nothing is more beautifully packed for the unfolding than bracken. How tender the tips were, curled in like babies' fingers!

Sycamore whistles could only be made when the sap was rising. I never had patience to make one for myself, but the boys made them. They would cut a length of sycamore shoot and ring two or three inches of the new skin—too delicate to be called bark—tap it with the handles of their penknives till it slipt off whole. Then they shaped the lip of the pipe, replaced the circular tube of skin, and the whistle would whistle if blown. I expect there was more to it than this, or why could I not make a whistle for myself? However, we whistled, and the birds sang—such larks there were—and the cuckoos cuckooed, and the flowers went in their great procession: from celandines to primroses and violets; from primroses and violets to bluebells and cuckooflowers with spotted leaves; from blackthorn to real may.

With the may came the Ascension and Whitsuntide. May was the name we gave to hawthorn. We had already nibbled the young leaves, green-cheese we called them, as they were unfolding from the buds on our thorn hedge; in autumn we should bite the haws and find them insipid. But with the flowers no fault could be found. We discovered quite soon in the game of putting flowers into families that they were akin to the rose. My mother would not have may in the house. Susan and I decorated for May Day and had junket and cream for 'lember'. We got out very early and decorated with what flowers we could find, and with fresh green boughs, before my mother was up. Although she must have heard us moving she always pretended great surprise when she came down and found the house a bower. Yes, she had completely forgotten it was May Day; no, we must have gone out like mice; never a sound had she heard; it was a lovely surprise and we were darlings.

Ascension Day came, a rather shorn festival, in spite of 'Hail the day that sees Him rise', for it was a week-day. But Whitsuntide, ten days later, was, next to Christmas Eve, my favourite day of the year. Would it be fine and warm enough for our white dresses? Otherwise there would again be trouble. Our friends would certainly wear their white dresses and straw hats unless it poured. Sometimes it was too early in the year, but Whitsuntides then were surely fine as a rule, or do I gild the weather? We sang 'Come, Holy Ghost, our souls inspire', 'Come, thou Holy Spirit, come' and 'Our Blest Redeemer'. The first was our favourite, but I had been taught the alto of 'Our Blest Redeemer'. Such voice as I had was low and it was delightful to me to be able to sing something without conking out on the top notes. I liked the Whitsuntide psalm, 'There go the ships and there is that Leviathan'—

Mevagissey fishing fleet and *The Queen of the Fal*
being chased by something akin to Jonah's whale.

Trinity Sunday was high summer. I once had
a new blue frock on Trinity Sunday, but only once.
Quite new frocks were extremely rare in my experience; Susan's frocks and Cap'n's jerseys descended
to me. My new blue frock is inextricably mingled
with 'Holy, holy, holy, Lord God Almighty'.
Mingled with it too are the blue of the sky, and the
blue sea at Hemmick with its glancing plates of
light. The saints were casting down their golden
crowns around that glassy sea. Loitering along the
lanes and fields to Horse Pool after church on
Whitsunday and Trinity was very delightful. Stitch-
wort would be out with little seed-cases to snap;
pink campion; and the first wild white roses; sweet
briar roses came later. We would hear Dart trotting
in the distance and then we would meet my father
and whoever had been to Caerhays with him, and
so home to the first gooseberry tart and cream.
Cream came from Agnes's in those days, lying yellow
as butter in a shallow wide glass dish.

Trinity is a festival of early June. The medieval
poet wrote:

> How lovesome thou art in May,
> Thou wide, wide earth.

Even more lovesome is the earth in June—leafy
June. If a person in possession of all his senses had
the luck to live on earth only a single Cornish June

he would, one would have thought, be thankful. What blaze of buttercups showering golden pollen on our shoes—buttercups topped with red sorrel; what waving silken grass; what dapple of light and shade through the leaves, what tangle of sweet briar in Treveor Hill. During the Sundays after Trinity, as the summer nights lengthened, my mother and Mrs. Kendal would walk for a longer and longer time after church in Cotna Lane. The two had been school friends and still loved each other. The Kendal children were our friends. There were nine of them: William, Janie, Lilian, Kathleen, Sybil, Jack, Phyllis, Joan and Edward. Jack and Phyllis were nearest in age to me. My mother would walk to Cotna with Mrs. Kendal, Mrs. Kendal would walk back with my mother, my mother would walk back with Mrs. Kendal . . . talking, talking they would go, while we disported ourselves round and about, anxious not to call attention to the fading light. Twilight is exciting even to machines; a motor bike will run with more zest as the light runs out. How much more exciting is it to children!

Hay harvest came. We went with our friends to different farms to watch and hinder rather than to help. The farmers were tolerant of children. Except for the Lawrys they all had children of their own. One or two of 'master's children' only swelled the rout. We watched the hay-cutter, played in the loose hay and round the cocks, rode in the empty wagons, and sometimes, with luck, on the top of a load. This was the greatest treat. We carried 'croust' to the workers, and had a little croust ourselves. At home we played at making hay in the garden. Our garden was by no means well kept. We let the grass get extra high in order to cut it and make hay. We raked and tossed and the scent of the sweet grass penetrated the house. 'Croust' was provided by my mother—cake and ginger pop, or herbie beer, or sherbet water. We carried our hay in the wheelbarrow, and made our rick on the three-cornered piece by the traphouse.

Hay harvest was often not in full swing until July, that is until after the longest day of the year. But it is with June I chiefly associate it; with the climax of the year's progression. In the rhythm of rise and fall which governs all things it is the rise which exhilarates. To mount, to reach the maximum height, to pause for an infinitesimal moment before the inevitable decline! I have heard that the soul can only float out of the body with the ebbing tide. The fall of the year, too, seems appropriate for a flitting. Who could die in the up-swing from January to June? In childhood one feels immortal all the year round; but even then June was, in some indefinable way, the highest pitch of the swing-boat.

6

FEASTS AND DIVERSIONS: GOING DOWN

I love my love in June for then
She wears a veil embroidered over
With sea-pink, columbine and clover.

I love my love in late September,
In the mellow sunshine when
Butterflies will illumine,

Like capitals on ancient scroll,
Her russet gown which must remember
Sobriety towards December.

I love my love in winter chill,
When the high winds hold festival
And furious the waves rise and roll.

But most I love my love in Spring,
When my bare feet upon the hill
Tread delicately the vernal squill,

And all the larks to heaven sing
This song my heart is carolling.

—To Cornwall in all Weathers

I CANNOT assign a month to Mevagissey regatta and Veryan show; they were, I think, in July or August. Other places had regattas but Mevagissey was the best as far as we were concerned—Fowey regatta was out of range for Dart. In the same way Veryan was the best of the flower shows. I remember Veryan show even more vividly than Mevagissey regatta. From Caerhays we went to the show year after year. It is connected in my mind with mazzards—little black cherries. At Caerhays we not only went to the show, but exhibited; though a third prize for sweet peas was all we ever won. Our gardening was too chancy for fatness.

A big disappointment to me in our first year at Caerhays was my failure in the children's wild flower competition. This prize I had marked down as my own. In the children's section of the printed list of desirable exhibits there was a notice which read something like this: 'A prize is offered for the best arranged bunch of wild flowers of any single variety.'

I was excited, for I fancied myself at arranging flowers. Susan who was more artistic could not compete; she was over twelve. I decided on a flower in which I greatly delighted at the time, partly because I had never noticed it growing round Gorran. The flower was centaury which grew on the Barns Hills. On stiff-looking erect stems the little flowers grew, stems very formally branched near the top, so that the petals, raying from fairy-like throats, were individually spaced and free. I thought their elegance would seduce any judge. I put only a few stems in my vase; I had an idea of displaying the separate geometry and colour of each of my chosen ones. I dreamt of that prize, and of seeing my flowers in the tent, more curiously lovely than all the others. The day arrived. My flowers had gone over with the other exhibits from Caerhays. As we were going to the show I gave the harness a special rub, and Dart a special grooming. I polished his hoofs with shoe polish. It used to be an extra-ordinarily lovely drive from Caerhays to Veryan. We went down the first and second hills beyond Caerhays Church, and turned left to Heras Water, where a clear stream ran across the road. Through the stream Dart had to wade; I was anxious for his polished hoofs. By the side of that stream, and all the way up the hill to Trevilveth, the most beautiful lacy ferns grew, and a delicately veined cranesbill, and a sorrel we called hare's meat. Veryan itself was a charming village much bigger than Caerhays, and more rural and leafy than Gorran. Susan and I wished we could live in one of the little round houses, each with its cross to scare the devil. There were four round houses; two and two they stood on either side of the road, guarding the entrances to Veryan. The show was held in a large field. A brass band would be playing fit to call the dead out of their graves for the dancing. Certainly such music would stir my poor scaffolding of bones. I was longing to know if I had a prize; but on the principle of 'Never seek to tell thy love', one aspect of which children understand so well, I said nothing. I wanted to go to the tent for myself and see my centiory honoured. But before we reached the tent-opening my friend, Alice Blandford, ran up and said, 'You haven't got no prize at all. Jimmy Martin's got un. Your bunch do look some funny'. The pang I felt at a failure in my first public examination was as nothing to the pang I felt for that centiory. I left my father and ran with Alice towards the tent. We squirmed our way through the crowd to the table where the children's exhibits were. The prize had rightly gone to Jimmy Martin's bowl of spear thistles. Thistles! I had despised them except for their silken down. Yet I have never seen any wild flowers look grander than those great fighting thistles. And far away in a corner, remote from the central splendour, was my centiory. I had never noticed that centiory closed its petals up in the absence of the sun. I had picked my bunch in bright sunlight; now it looked some funny as Alice had said. The next year in imitation of the bold democratic choice of Jimmy Martin I tried horse-daisies, but Jimmy won the prize with plumes of meadow-sweet. The year after that we were both too old to compete. Clever Jimmy Martin—his mother called him James—he became a gardener like his father, and played with flowers all his life. Very grand prizes have come his way since those days.

In addition to flowers in the tent there were fatted

vegetables and fruits. We cared little for these. We made for the live stock. In their pens and hutches rabbits and puppies, and even cocks and hens had a smart strange appearance. It was like meeting well-known relatives in their best clothes at a party. We would stare in at the bulls. 'Bulls that walk the pastures in kingly-flashing coats' were fearful in our eyes. I never in my life saw a bull at large without making for the nearest hedge. 'To be horned' was our equivalent to being bombed. 'He'll horn ee', folk would say to frighten us when a bull was in the mowy. At the show we could look at the necks of the Red Devons from safe ground.

In the afternoon there was a horse-show and bicycle racing. Cart-horses, their manes and tails wonderfully tricked out, their coats sleek in the sun, would pace obediently but proudly. They seemed to restrain the power in their deliberate heavy stepping simply to indulge the little men who led them. Their submission was as though voluntary and not shameful, for they had strength to cast off any yoke if they liked to exert it. Their strength made them sure of themselves. Cart-horses never show off. They are the equivalent in horse-life to Conrad's favourite type of hero in human kind, creatures of great integrity who will do their duty in spite of the fury of the elements, and the wiles of gods and women. The high-stepping carriage horses who went round the ring looked self-conscious and flashy in comparison, but I loved them.

Best of all was the jumping. I have never had the luck to see much horse-racing, but it is an intelligible passion. There is an interesting short story by D. H. Lawrence called 'The Rocking Horse Winner', one of the little moralities he enjoyed writing. It is the story of a child living in a house which whispered, 'There must be more money, there must be more money'. His mother said luck was better than fortune. He knew that his rocking horse could take him to where there was luck (lucre) for his mother if he forced it. So he would sit on his rocking horse charging wildly until he reached Luck and a certain intuition as to which horse would win in a race. 'Sansovino' he would find at the end of his journey; Sansovino; Daffodil, Lively Spark. Sometimes he would ride and never reach Luck. He would not be sure. Then he and Basset, the young gardener enthusiast, would go lightly; but when he knew, when he was *sure*, they would go strong, they would go for all they were worth. The story ends with the child being interrupted by his mother in the ritual of the furious mad riding of the rocking horse. But he had reached Luck. He dies in a brain fever, but not until he has whispered 'Malabar' and made other people's fortunes by his own death.

There was no proper horse-racing at Veryan show, but the bicycle racing had, in its small way, the thrill which has been exploited by the flicks. Set one person or animal chasing or racing another and we are haled out of ourselves into the pursuit. I was watching John Gielgud's production of *Macbeth* in the gods of a theatre not long ago. Two small boys were near me. They stood up and watched the final mêlée. Macbeth went out left; Macduff came in right as though in hot pursuit, chasing him. 'That way, mister', the smaller boy yelled. It was the first time in the play he had been utterly caught away into the performance.

In August and September we often tended to set out with baskets and bags for picking this and that. I did not much like the picking, but I enjoyed the accessories. It has been suggested to me that in order to inculcate the virtues of steadiness and patience one might be put through a course of fruit-picking, beginning with 'urts'. There were no urts (whortleberries) near us. We picked mushrooms, blackberries, sloes and nuts. I liked mushrooming best of all, the basket filled so quickly, and the mushrooms seemed to grow like magic. They were an incentive, too, to get out early and taste the freshness of the day. The dewy twinklings and mares' tails would be like watering-cans, drenching our legs, as we made our way over fields to the good places. Rainy heat is the weather for mushrooms, soft warm rain, and enough heat to soak into fields unbroken by the plough and grazed by horses. Land need not be in good heart to produce mushrooms; indeed the more heartless the land the better the crop. 'I spy a mushroom' was the cry of the first person to strike a silken button or spreading umbrella. Sometimes we would be deceived and go haring after toadstools or puffballs. We made no experiments in cooking fungi. Mushrooms we knew and these we stuck to. We liked them with delicate pink gills, but we picked the older ones too, those with gills grown dark, almost black. Sometimes when we had miscalculated the weather, or were too early in the year, we would walk far and find nothing. But in the really fruitful season we would pile baskets high with mushrooms of all sizes; our fingers stained and smelling of mushrooms. We would try to get home in time to have fried mushrooms with our bacon for breakfast. I liked skinning them; the skin came off in fascinating strips, leaving the mushrooms soft white like shorn lambs with pink showing through the white.

Blackberrying was, as often as not, a whole day's business. In our oldest clothes we set out with a big basket or two, together with a cup or mugs or jugs for each picker. Agnes's Moors, which lay between us and Gorran Haven, grew wonderful big blackberries, for the moors were damp and reedy and the bushes big. The juiciest looking berries always seemed to be almost inaccessible, tempting us to press on regardless of scratches and rents. I never felt the scratches until afterwards, when seeing them made me feel them. In the tangled thickets would be great white woodbine cups, white even to the anthers and stigma; sprays of honey-suckle; late bramble flowers like painted ragged girls; and the green, red, and ripe blackberries. The members of the party would spread out, each trying to find a special pocket for himself, and fill his cup with big berries to make the tide in the basket mount high as the filled cups were poured into it. Sometimes we went as far as Dodman. But it was in the valleys, the 'bottoms' as we say in Cornwall, that the sensuous blackberry spell was strongest. There Pan was near. The pickers with purple-stained mouths and fingers were his subjects. So were the bullocks who sometimes went half mad in the heat, and careered wildly, forgetting all their placid cud-chewing. We would say they had the wop, and sometimes had an attack of something resembling the wop ourselves. Perhaps it was due to the hornets or the sun; I have heard the gorse-pods pop in the heat.

In September we picked sloes and bullums (bullaces) for our wine. Doughty mentions as a faery drink, 'last year's bullaces laid up in honey'; smoothly intoxicating it sounds, gliding down the gullet. We laid our bullaces up in sugar. We never managed to secure any gin. This making of sloe wine was a children's affair though my mother pro-vided us with sugar and bottles. Sloes looked so

tempting with the purple-misty bloom on them that
I always tried to eat one or two and rasped my teeth.
As one bites through the skin to the ungenerous
green pulp, which scantily covers a stone too
big for it, the watering mouth is dried up with
bitterness. Thorns and the harsh fruit match one
another. But how lovely the blossom is, appearing
before the leaves, close to the blackthorn; life break-
ing in full flush from what seems winter-dead! It
is the right spring blossom for the Cornish cliffs,
reinforcing a contrast already existing. The virtue
of all flowers, their ardent fragility, is heightened
by the stubbornness from which they spring.

Nutting was the most hilarious of all our expedi-
tions, partly because it happened only once. We
went blackberrying and mushrooming many times
in a season, but our store of nuts usually depended
on one Saturday's picking in Scotland wood. Grown-
ups went nutting with us. We carried crooked sticks
and bags, and went by Menagwins, Churchtown,
Cotna Lane, Cotna, Sentries and so into Scotland
wood with its deep rutty lane lined with hazels. As
we walked bits of stick crackled and fallen leaves
rustled under foot. Rich dyes coloured the bramble
and the rose. Here was the birds' harvest of berries,
aglets, and scarlet rose-hips, strings of bryony,
bright jack-in-the-pulpit, the luscious looking red
fruits of the honeysuckle and woody-nightshade.
We picked up beech nuts to string together for

necklaces, and smooth acorns and oakers to play with. We climbed and swung on the trees. But most of our attention was given to the hazels on which the nuts grew in clusters, each nut in a cup with a frilled edging. When nuts slipped the cup easily they were ripe. The texture of the hazel shell takes colour smoothly; its green and fawn have given a name to one of the colours in the human eye. We have not a beech or lime or an oaken eye; only hazel. Ripe nuts were riper in colour. It is a pity we do not plant more hazel. Too many conifers are being planted in Cornwall because of their quick growth. But hazel, beech and birch; ash, oak, elm, thorn, holly and sycamore are more suitable to our Roseland. Larch plantations with their spring tufts of light green and their rose-coloured fresh cones fit the landscape better than fir and pine which are dour and Scotch. Spruce is unfitting.

Sweet chestnuts grew moderately well. We picked up our chestnuts in the castle drive and usually got a fair number. But they did not grow large and lusty like the horse chestnuts, for they were often blown down before the nuts were ripe. As they came out of their cosy lined home they looked flatish and puny, in white and brown with silky hairs at the tip, as though not properly out of their milk-teeth; whereas the horse chestnuts burst out of their more commonplace cases red-brown, plump and handsome. We valued horse-chestnuts as much if not

more than the sweet ones. Of them we made dolls'
furniture, particularly chairs. We stuck in four
stout pins for legs and three pins for a back; the
chestnut made the seat. Then we wound coloured
wool round the pin-legs and wove wool through the
three pins at the back. Thus in a short time a set
of elegant mahogany chairs could be completed.
But more valuable still were horse-chestnuts for
conkers. Some conkers, polished and hardened,
and preserved with care, became the real old men
of the tribe, absolute king conkers; till they, after
proving themselves invincible in a whole village of
inferior conkers, went the way of all tyrants and
were split by some young strong upstart.

By September the village was ready to praise God
for the harvest. Sometimes we praised Him too soon
and sang that all was safely gathered in before it was.
But we knew that God would understand. No need
to explain to Him that the day for the harvest
festival had been fixed some weeks ago and that
though Mr. Kendal, Mr. Nott, Mr. Mitchel,
Mr. Lawry and Mr. Lanyon had done their best,
what with the weather and one thing and another,
they hadn't quite managed. A few shocks still out.
I have no patience with the modern scrupulous
revisers of hymns who limit God's benevolent understanding of His people's little exaggerations and
subterfuges. I see that in 'Hymns of Praise' the
old 'All is safely gathered in' is altered to 'All be

safely gathered in', and that there is some hanky-panky with Mrs. Alexander's 'Rushes by the water, we gather every day'. The literal-minded were worried because we no longer gather rushes every day. Really, really! As though God would stumble over a little thing like that.

We rejoiced in the harvest in a way best expressed in Hopkins' 'Hurrahing for Harvest'. Barbarous in beauty the stooks arise. My heart leapt to it when I first read those words. Harvest festivals, though somewhat disparaged by Churchmen as upstart services with little tradition, were the most popular church festivals of the year when I was a child. Men seemed to come together with more willingness to express praise and gratitude than to bewail their sins and consider how fearful it was to fall into the hands of the living God. People went round to different parishes to harvest festivals, and chapel people went to church and church people to chapel. We did not seem to mind how often we sang 'We plough the fields and scatter', 'Now thank we all our God', 'Come, ye thankful people, come', 'For His mercies still endure, ever faithful, ever sure', and 'All people that on earth do dwell, Sing to the Lord with cheerful voice'. The first time we ever chanted a psalm in my memory in Gorran church was at a Harvest Festival. Usually we said the psalms, the Vicar reading one verse and the congregation the next, and so on to the end when we sang a Gloria. But for one harvest festival we chanted 'O praise God in His Holiness; praise Him in the firmament of His power'. By the time we reached 'Let everything that hath breath praise the Lord', I had got the hang of it and was so loud in praise that Mr. Jorey, the blacksmith who shod our pony, and who would let us blow the bellows, turned round and gave me a peppermint.

Harvest was the least liturgical, the most pagan festival of the year. Even the decorations rioted. Dahlias would never go to church by nature; whereas lilies might have been born in church. Golden wheat-ears, dahlias, crimson virginia creeper, vegetable marrows, pumpkins, apples, bunches of grapes, in coming to church changed the church's character, not their own. They laughed in all their expansive richness. The parish feasted in common at Harvest Festival, but not at Christmas, Easter, Whitsuntide, or Trinity. There was no parish tea except at Harvest. Sitting on forms, at trestle tables, we drank tea from thick white cups and ate buttered splits, saffron cake, sultana cake, and jam-and-cream splits. I think kiss-in-the-ring was seldom played except at harvest festivals. Already when I was a child people were shy of it, whereas it had been popular when my mother was a girl. She would tell us how in her day, too, as it grew to twilight the games had ceased; the bells had rung for the

evening service, and church and chapel folk had
sung together, 'Let everything that hath breath
praise the Lord'. Gladness is generous and uniting.
According to Baring Gould, the Rev. Stephen
Hawker was the first to institute a harvest festival
in the Cornish Church. In 1843 he sent a notice
to his parishioners at Morwenstow saying that as
in that year God had opened His hand and filled all
things living with plenteousness the people should
meet together on the first Sunday in October to
offer a sacrifice of thanksgiving. They would receive
at the sacrament bread made of the new corn. By
my time the festival was less truly religious, but
hardly less joyful. Joy, however, seems to decline
as the religious motive recedes. Mere conviviality
is not life to the spirit.

With the gold of October came bonfires, and the
smell of smoke, as we burnt the garden trash and
baked potatoes in the ashes. We lit our fires in
the evening as the light was falling. Fire was the
autumn God, 'bona-firies, their red beards streaming to the heavens'. We kindled fires furtively and
in the open. Cap'n and I raced flames down dry
sticks. The pointed triangular sails of flame were
our fire-ships. We could make little fires in the
coalhouse at night, for it was Cap'n's job to pick up,
in readiness for the morning, wood and coal for the
kitchen fire. I would go out to help him with his
labour. Then on the stone floor we would burn

a little paper, a few sticks, and pellets of candle-grease. Cap'n would try sprinkling a little sugar, salt, sulphur, or copper filings to change the colours. We would have green flames and yellow, edged with mauve or blue. The coalhouse was next the washhouse—both across the court from the dwelling house. Absorbed in our pleasure we would forget time stealing by until a voice would call from the back door, 'What are you children doing over there?' We would guiltily extinguish our little fires and hasten in with an armful of dry wood and our lumps of coal broken up into suitable sizes for lighting the kitchen range.

Near Guy Fawkes day we experimented with squibs and sparklers, just one or two to make sure they were not damp. Once Stan and a friend made some gunpowder, or got it from cartridges, I am not sure which. They set it in a hedge and laid a fuse. But the fuse did not go off when they thought it should. They drew near to see what was wrong and as they were about to bend over it off it went. Stan's eyebrows and hair were singed, he looked a funny sight. He had black marks in his face. He went to Howard and asked what he could do to himself so that my mother should not see. Howard suggested washing. This had a frightful heightening effect. There was nothing for it. Stan's burnt state was plain to all, but he had hurt himself too much already for parental retribution.

Our store of fireworks was always small for we had little money; but we made a guy and had a splendid bonfire. There would be a tarred faggot and driftwood with banners of flame; then as the yellow sheets furled themselves we would poke the ashes into sparks and feed our fire with furze. The consuming flowers would break fiery among the spines, swiftly ablaze, and swiftly in ashes, lighting and dying. Later from our bedroom windows we used to watch the rockets going up over Mevagissey, rockets rushing upwards, and bursting into floating flakes and spangles of light.

There is no Feast of Lights or Feast of Fires in the Church. In November came All Saints' Day. We sang 'How bright these glorious spirits shine' and 'For all the saints who from their labours rest'. But I could never love the saints nor care for Heaven. Until I was grown up, and knew Vaughan and Crashaw, Herbert and Hopkins, my joys were purely earthly. Even my delight in the great Church festivals was, I think, in looking back, more an unconscious passion for Cornwall than for the Church. When I recall Gorran Church or Caerhays Church they are always part of the weather and of the fields and the sky; rain on the roof; trees at Gorran moving their branches outside the un-painted east window; sun streaming in at the open door at Caerhays; the sound of birds chirping or singing during the quiet parts of the service; a red admiral fluttering between the pillars. At Caerhays one could even hear the bees humming over the self-heal and knapweed and clover, and the grasshoppers rattling their brackeny shanks. No doubt I forget how often as a child I was bored in church. Kneeling through the Litany I would long to be out of 'Good Lord deliver us' and into 'We beseech thee to hear us, Good Lord', a response which went on interminably. I would press my hands against my eyes so as to make violet and yellow geometrical patterns float against the blackness; or I would squint through my eyelashes at a rainbow-edged Miss Ellen Wills. She kept the post office and came into church walking on her toes. 'O Lord who at this time with one accord', Mr. Sowel would say at last, and I knew I should soon stand up. 'O Lord, who at this time' and 'And now to God the Father . . .' which ended the sermon, were words I sometimes longed for to the extent of trying to conjure them out of the distance.

Yet, though not a naturally religious child, I am glad I was taken to church regularly, initiated into the Christian faith, and helped to participate in the profound poetry of the Christian year. Though inattentive I came insensibly to know the liturgy word for word, and to live in the double rhythm of the earthly seasons and of man's noblest imagining. After the fall of the year, came the pause, the hush of waiting in field and church, and Advent Sunday.

The Collect for Advent Sunday was the first Collect
for the day I was set to learn by heart. I was very
proud to be out of the Catechism and into the
Collects with Susan and the boys. I determined to
be word perfect. We said the Collect to my mother
on Sunday mornings. It was not easy to learn and
nothing was explained—excessive explanation is the
wicked fairy in modern education. For me there
was no tarnishing progress; the rhythmic prose
swung unchipped into my mind:

'Almighty God, give us grace that we may cast
away the works of darkness, and put upon us the
armour of light, now in the time of this mortal life,
in which Thy Son Jesus Christ came to visit us in
great humility; that in the last day, when He shall
come again in His glorious majesty to judge both
the quick and the dead, we may rise to the life
immortal. Through Him who livest and reignest with
Thee and the Holy Ghost, now and ever. Amen.'

I did not know how grand it was, I was only
exultant that I was learning it. I shouted it to the
thorns and to the wind; and my mother, when I
repeated it on Sunday, said it was good.

7

VISITING

Unmoored,
   Lifting,
Into the space
   Drifting.

No steersman now
   Save sweet delight
Dreaming with me
   All night.
            —*On Falling Asleep*

THERE were some houses which we were in and out of so often that we could not be called visitors. Of these were Cotna and Trevesan where there were children matching us in age. When I think of Gorran I feel as homesick for Cotna as for the School House. Taking the church as the centre of the village Cotna lay in the opposite direction from the School House. On leaving church we went down the granite steps under the cross by the old sun-dial, and so home. The Kendals went past the oldest old tombstones, and down the darker, romantic, shallow slate steps at the back of the churchyard into their own lane, which curved along between hedges into what we called the Oval.

I have heard my mother say that at one time the Oval used to be shaven as smooth as the Vicarage lawn. In our day it was wilder grass, and the plantations round it were wild too. Crocuses, yellow and purple, and clumps of daffodils came up unattended in the spring. In June there were scented roses called blush roses for their flushing crimson petals, velvety to touch. We used to stick petals on our foreheads, rose petals and geranium. In the orchard there were medlar trees; no other orchard had the rotten-ripe medlars. As for the house it was the house I should best like to live in in the world. It had a straight front with straight sash windows on either side of a portico with pillars. Upstairs one could get on to the portico from what was called the blue room.

Here lived Mr. Kendal, known throughout the parish as Cap'n Bill to distinguish him from his brothers Freeman and Leonard who farmed Bodrugan and Trewollack. With him was Mrs. Kendal whom next to my own family, and perhaps Miss Mary of the Barley Sheaf, I chiefly loved. I once read a poem about how the birds slept sweetly all night at their mother's side. Mrs. Kendal might almost have had feathers. She was essentially a person to nestle against, immobile; the very antithesis of angularity and restlessness. She moved little, walking always slowly and in one; she did not turn her head about or move her arms separately from herself. She had an easy way, a softness I have never met in an equal degree in anybody else. For her to raise her voice or speak in a sharp tone would have been impossible. The babies might yell; the older children, strong and handsome, be on the rampage; the work accumulate; the meals be running feasts—she remained placid. She always came to church late, walking quietly in, sometimes during the Venite, sometimes even as late as the Second Lesson. The quickening stroke of the 'last bell' which hastened other footsteps never hastened Mrs. Kendal's. Unflurried, never looking late, she would enter the church innocently; making it seem not as though she were late but as though we had all come foolishly early. Cap'n Bill would be already in place, for he was a ringer and a Churchwarden. Standing upright at the end of the Kendal's seat, and looking at his prayer-book, he would feel instinctively her approach, but would not take his eyes from his book, or interrupt his song if we were in song. He would merely step into the aisle, and she would pass by him into her place. She would then go in, kneel down for her little private prayer, stand up, look up with a slight smile at Cap'n Bill, find her place in her book and dissolve into the congregation. In all she did she was entirely herself. Perhaps her secret was that she never tried to dominate or chase anything, and so nothing resisted her or ran away from her. She had no pursuits.

Her clothes were her familiars. Her plush jacket was Mrs. Kendal, not Mrs. Kendal's jacket; it seemed as much a part of her as her brown eyes. She was the only person who called my mother Sue. Bessie and Sue they had been to each other as schoolgirls and so remained. My father called my mother Dan'l—her full Christian name was Susan Daniel—after a character in a book called Dan'l Quorm.

Cap'n Bill Kendal was in many ways a contrast to his wife, but he was good natured too. He used to get me to say I loved him two great apples. I only once made him angry. Jack Kendal and I had ensconced ourselves in the interior of a great yew tree on the Oval. We found that if we climbed up the limbs of the tree from inside we reached a point at which our weight was too great for the limb. It swayed outwards giving us a gentle yet breath-taking swing nearly to the ground, when we dropped off, and repeated the process with another limb. Entirely wrapt in our delighted sensations we never gave a thought to the tree till Cap'n Bill was on us. He caught and cuffed Jack, and would have cuffed me too if I'd been one of my brothers. I instantaneously saw the tree through his eyes, and I fear the Judgment will be to see the effect of one's whole life with unhooded eyes as I saw that tree. Previously I had been unconscious of the tree except as an object providing us with a game. Now I saw that instead of being a tree with a great wide base and all its limbs curving up to a point, the yew had limbs which had not sprung back into place, but which were rudely wrenched outward. Cap'n Bill shouted at us how old the tree was; I forget how many years old, hundreds of years it seemed. He said it was the finest yew in Cornwall. I think it was the first time I had ever been sorry for a thing I had hurt, as apart from being sorry for myself because of what was happening to me for hurting it. Similar absorptions of mine had been vigorously interrupted when I was small, but then I had merely felt furiously angry. I can remember what must have been the one absolute and genuine artistic absorption of my life. I had got a little bit of slate— there were many sharp flat slate stones about—and I was making marks with it on the highly polished surface of a cupboard. All my self was in the point of the slate. To be caught out of the trance, and slapped, and made to realize it was a cupboard I was spoiling, was to pass from one world abruptly into another. But I was sorry for myself, not for the cupboard. Similarly, when I was making a hole in the traphouse in order to have an inner cave like Robinson Crusoe, I hadn't made it big enough for me to crawl through before I was caught; but it was a hole big enough for the Plymouth Rocks to pass through and roost (on our trap)—with nasty results to the navy blue upholstering. Other animals crept through that hole till William Smith had to come and mend it. But I was never sorry for the traphouse. I was sorry for the yew tree, which had to be put as it were in splints. Stakes were driven into the earth and rope tied round to make the yew limbs grow up once more.

Trevesan, like Cotna, was nearly a second home. We envied Gordon, Louise and Stella Whetter for living nearer Hemmick than we did, and for having flavoured treacle on their bread-and-butter for tea. Mrs. Whetter—her Christian name was Petronella—let them have treacle of a raspberry or strawberry flavour and coloured red; whereas our treacle at home was ordinary. We did not count it 'going out to tea' to go to Trevesan or Cotna, or to school friends in the village. Going out to tea proper was when two or three of us went by set invitation with our parents to rather more distant friends—to the Mitchels at Penare, to the Mingos at Rescassa, to the Pearces at Tregerrick, or to our distant cousins, the Notts and Grosses, at Trevarrick. Other Nott relations lived at Bosinver and Coyte in St. Mewan parish. My favourite of all places to which to go formally to tea was Trevasgas where the Wests lived. We nearly always drove to Trevasgas; it was rather far for my mother to walk. At Trevasgas lived Mr. and Mrs. West, Percy, who soon farmed Trevennen on his own, Blanche, Martin, Sam and Norman. Blanche was just grown-up, and

Susan and I had all the little girl's admiration for the newly-arrived young woman. Blanche West was tall with smooth chestnut hair 'done-up', and a complexion a queen might envy. On arriving at Trevasgas we were taken to the spare bedroom which was Susan's delight, so unlike was it to anything in our own house. The boards of the floor were not stained; they kept their natural colour with a satin sheen; while on either side of the bed, in front of the fireplace, and in front of the dressing-table, were snowy sheep-fleeces. Susan yearned for a sheep fleece. I gave her one in later years, but it lacked the Trevasgas white silk curliness. There the fleeces were more than the depth of one's fingers. As a farmer said to me once, when I was looking at his prize living ewe, 'Feel her fleece, Anne, feel the depth of 'un'. In addition to the fleeces Trevasgas spare bedroom had white muslin curtains tied with pink bows, and a dressing-table in skirts. It wore a shiny pink under-skirt, and a clear-muslin, full-gathered overskirt. There were more pink bows, not creased like our hair ribbons, but fresh, crisp, newly tied bows. Except for maidenhair ferns in pots I cannot remember how the downstair rooms were furnished, but there was a back as well as a front staircase, and an open fire with a chimney corner in the kitchen.

We would help to feed the animals, or hunt for eggs, or play hide-and-seek about the barn and mowy until we were called in to a resplendent tea. The Wests' dining table was long and wide, covered with starched white damask. The food was choicely dispersed here and there on dishes set with d'oyleys. Some d'oyleys had wide-dropping crocheted or knitted lace. Some d'oyleys were goffered. The flowers on the centre varied with the season, but I see them as tulips; circling round the tulips on the d'oyleys would be thin bread and butter, yeast splits for cream and jam, rocky buns, sponge cake, saffron cake or fruit cake and, as the supreme triumph, the last point to work up to—tipsy cake. Tipsy cake was home-made sponge cake soaked in sherry, covered with stiff whipped cream, and studded with blanched almonds and cherries. Sometimes sponge fingers also stuck up on the top. I don't know what the grown-ups did, but traditionally the children ate solidly from the bread and butter base through all the varied delicacies to the top of the pyramid—the tipsy cake. Had I confessed the truth I should have owned that, once the cherries, the almonds, the whipped cream, and the sponge fingers were eaten, I did not like the harsh woody-bitter taste of the winey cake. But I never did own it. Susan did; that was the difference between us. She never pretended she could see a ship through a coastguard's telescope if she could not.

In summer after tea we played again out of doors. In winter we played blind-man's-buff in the kitchen.

The grown-ups then had supper in the dining-room, but Blanche got the children's supper in the kitchen. I would sit in the chimney corner and drink the hot cocoa which Blanche poured from a jug, and eat biscuits with smooth white or pink sugar on the top, or sugar in wavy designs. Once Blanche got us biscuits like animals. Then sleep would come at me. Fought from my eyes it would come stealing in from all sides through my body. The cold air, as we went out of the lighted room to drive home in the dark, would wake me thoroughly; but once in the trap, and snuggled for safety against my mother, I would surrender. I would give up protesting that it wasn't past my bed-time and float into sleep.

At Tregerrick I remember not so much the food—except the Polly apples—as the games. The Pearces were all grown up, but they played games in such a way as to make them furiously exciting. Ludo, tiddleywinks, hoop-la, snakes and ladders, snap, old maid, steeple-chasers—the Pearces had kept all the games they had had as children, and played them again with us, not in a bored way, but as if winning were the end of life. Ludo at the Pearces was utterly unlike Ludo anywhere else. Janey and Annie Pearce, and even Mrs. Pearce, would play. It was a life and death matter to throw a six and 'get out'. We yelled our disappointment when 'knocked home'. My sister-in-law has sometimes reproached me when playing with her children; she says I make them boisterous. The Pearces were like that, they made us boisterous, bless them.

The farthest distance we drove for an afternoon visit was to my Great-uncle Tommy's. He lived at a farm called Penvose, not very far from Portloe, where he would have it that the Jacka was the finest bit of cliff in Cornwall. He was a Wesleyan local preacher, with confidence in the efficacy of an ejaculated Amen. He always said a long grace before tea. He would clasp his hands, the fingers interlacing, and place them so as to make a little porch to his eyes. Then he would say:

> Be present at our table, Lord,
> Be here and everywhere adored,
> These creatures bless, and grant that we
> May rest in Paradise with Thee.

We would wait a minute with our heads bowed till Uncle Tommy in his preaching voice said Amen, Amen, A-Amen. Then he would add in his brisk ordinary Cornish tones, as of one relieved that his dues to heaven were paid, 'Now, my dears, fall to'. Apple tart and cream we had at Uncle Tommy's, summer or winter. He kept apples till apples came again. The apple tart was not made in a pie dish but had pastry top and bottom. The top would be taken off, sugar and cream inserted, and the top put on again. Despising the nursery rite of the tea-table, Uncle Tommy would begin straight away with apple tart, and proceed as it were backward and downward, through saffron cake to bread and butter.

While we lived at Gorran, to go to tea with the Martins and the Sargents at the Hovel was visiting. But when we lived at Caerhays we went to the Hovel so often that it ceased to count as visiting. Mr. Sargent was the head gamekeeper at Caerhays. He and Mrs. Sargent were already between sixty and seventy when I first remember them. Mrs. Sargent was the only person in the two parishes who wore a little lace cap and a black satin apron in the afternoons. She had, too, a little three-cornered red shawl to keep the draught from the small of her back. Their sons had gone out into the world but their daughters, Ellen and Frank (Frances), lived at home, where Ellen did dressmaking. From living long together Mr. and Mrs. Sargent had grown curiously alike in feature and in mind. They had a homely and accustomed goodness; it would have been impossible to connect them with any mean act or even thought. 'Cleanse the thoughts of our hearts by the inspiration of Thy Holy Spirit' they had prayed Sunday after Sunday after Sunday until there was no squalor in them. Their cottage was perfect, thatched as I first remember it, but later the thatch—the Squire had a dread of fire— was replaced by tiles. Mr. Sargent was a more travelled person than most of us. Every year he went to Scotland with Mr. Williams. He would tell us how once on Crewe station, where he was on guard with the dogs and the guns, a thief, not observing him, had stalked off with a gun. 'I went after him, and I said, "Why have you taken that gun?" I said. "That's my master's gun," I said . . .' We would poke the old man up to tell this story, again and again. I can see him in his fawn suit with pockets of pattern peculiar to himself, and wearing his neat gaiters, carrying his gun, and fawned on by obedient dogs. A badly trained dog would have dishonoured him. He was deeply distressed when a red setter called Mac once nipped into our kitchen and stole our Sunday joint. Mrs. Sargent considered that everyone should save a little money, however small the amount coming in. She was scandalized at the improvidence of Mevagissey folk, their poverty in bad times, and their extravagance in good. She liked sober dressing. 'Ha'penny head and farthing tail', she would say of somebody wearing a fine new flower-trimmed hat, and down-at-heel shoes. When I first began to earn a salary, and came home for holidays, I always hastened down to see the Sargents on my first night at home. Mrs. Sargent was much concerned that I, not being frugally inclined, and my earnings being small, was putting nothing into the savings bank. 'Now Anne, my dear, haven't ee put anything by yet?' she would say each time I came home. She would shake her head over my thriftlessness. Once when I told her how I had tried dividing my monthly salary into four parts and putting the four parts into four drawers of my bureau, so much for each week, and how by the end of the third week I had borrowed to such an extent from the fourth drawer that I had nothing left to live on, she laughed, but disapprovingly. When she was really amused her laughter used to begin with a quaking movement which lifted her folded hands up and down on her stomach; then it worked upwards through her heaving bosom until she wiped the tears from her eyes. Once to please her I put a pound into the Post Office Savings Bank; but Susan came to stay with me for a weekend. On the Friday evening I took ten shillings out to celebrate; on the Saturday I took the other ten shillings out to celebrate further. Mrs. Sargent, when told this story, said she must give me up for lost. Anyone who would do that would never save money however much she earned. She spoke the truth.

But it was Susan who lost our very first bit of capital. I must have been about seven years old and for the first time we were going away from home to stay. We had got between us, by some manner of means, the enormous sum of five shillings. It was the summer we were wearing cream serge sailor-suits and cream yachting caps. Susan put our fortune in a purse in the pocket of her 'top'. We were tremendously excited, for I had never been anywhere by train before. Cap'n warned me not to go too near the edge of the platform; the train, he said, would seem to get me by the gizzard, and draw me towards it. And indeed it did. When the monster came rushing towards me out of St. Austell rhododendron bushes, and I felt its breath on my face, and the tug which Cap'n had foretold at my middle, I clutched the person nearest me. Afterwards, when teased, I said I only clutched the person for fun; I was ashamed because it was not even an express train. We had, for my benefit, chosen a train which would stop at all the little stations— Burngullow, Grampound Road, Probus Halt and Truro. At Truro we changed into the Falmouth train and got out at Perranwell. The name of the station was growing in candytuft on one of the station flower-beds. Again Cap'n had told me what to expect, and there it was. I determined to plant ANNE in pansies, but I never did.

Several of my father's relations lived round about Perran-ar-Worthal. We were to stay at Poplar and were met at the station by one of my cousins in the Poplar trap. We were in high feather, with no thought of impending mischance, when I began to tell my cousin Tom how we had five shillings between us to spend. Susan clapt her hand to her 'top' pocket, and alas, it was empty. That purse had hopped out. From being independent persons with a fortune to spend, we found ourselves in a condition of abject poverty, for my father refused to give us another ha'penny. I was not magnanimous to Susan over our loss. I said, in bed, that if I'd had my own share of the five shillings it wouldn't have hopped out of my 'top' pocket; Susan, conscious of guilt, and so contentious, said I wasn't to be trusted with even a decent pocket-handkerchief. Where was that little hemstitched handkerchief with lace edging which Aunt Lye had sent me two Christmases ago? And who had broken her scent bottle? I had a passion for scent and, essaying to steal Susan's one day, I had broken a unique bottle of carnation which had a tiny ivory pump handle and spout at the top of it. Other old offences we threw at each other from the past; we lay in bed back to back. But we could never go to sleep 'vexed'; besides I was beginning to feel lonely. I knew that 'I'm feeling lonely' would always make Susan turn towards me however much she might be striving to nourish her anger. I said the words now, and we turned towards each other. What was five shillings!

Probably it was five shillings well lost, for the high light of our visit was Penryn regatta, where I had my first ice-cream and my first ride on the roundabouts. With thirty pennies of my own to spend I should probably have joined the angels. No ambrosia will ever taste so ambrosial as that first ha'penny ice-cream wafer bought off the ice-cream cart of an Italian, with ear-rings.

> Oh, Oh, Antonio.   He's gone away.
> Left me alonio.   All on my ownio.

I hardly watched the yachts at all. What with ice-cream and the roundabouts my cup of bliss was already full. The blare of the music, and those horses, so dashing in their bridles, moving in two ways at once, up and down, and round about! My cousin Tom treated me, and together we went lilting. Holding my reins, I sat side-saddle like Miss Williams at the castle who never rode astride. I think it gave me a vague notion of what I was missing through not riding Dart side-saddle, and wearing a long habit. A long-skirted riding habit, like a long, rustling party dress, must change one's nature.

I liked my cousin Alfred Harry. I sat next him in Ponsanooth chapel where we 'leaned vor' instead of kneeling down in the church way. In one of the long prayers, while the preacher was venturing to remind Almighty God of this and that, and while we were 'leaning vor' Alfred Harry, to my inexpressible apprehension and shocked delight, drew with a pin a funny face on the varnished pew. He had a funny face himself and could move his ears.

Various friends and relations returned visits to the School House, but my mother was too impatient to run to d'oyleys. She said our dishes were too good to hide. The party of ours I most vividly remember in my earliest years was a concert-party supper. Sammy Rowe of Mevagissey had brought his band to play at a concert in Gorran School, and he and the others were to have supper in our house before going home through the dark. Susan was playing a duet with Howard at the concert, so it was I who had the splendour of helping my mother with the final touches to the supper table. By the time we were ready to slip into our seats in the schoolroom the band was already under way. I shall never forget treading on air to those sounds. The fiddlers had lifted their bows, and Sammy was intoxicating himself with the cornet. He was a true musician. Once in later days, so I have heard, Sammy was playing his cornet and leading the band round Mevagissey quay, when he stepped clean over the jetty in his ecstasy; but the air refused to bear him up; he had to be pulled out of the water, dripping wet, the divine frenzy quenched. At Mevagissey Feast, St. Peter's Day, there always used to be a procession to the sea.

Visiting was a favourite game with Susan and me on wet winter Saturday afternoons. We called this game 'young ladies'. Susan would have our bedroom, I would have the boys' bedroom—the

boys being safely out rabbiting with my father at
Beeparks. We would divide the dolls and get out
our tea-sets. Then we dressed up in mother's clothes
or in long dresses made of old curtains. We turned
out discarded veils and jet bracelets, and carried old
sunshades with deep fringes. We then took turns
to visit each other, knocking at each other's doors,
being admitted, being taken to the equivalent of the
spare bedroom to remove our veils, and sitting down
sometimes to an imaginary tea, sometimes, if mother
were in a good mood, to real little bits of cake, and
a mock blanc-mange made of moist sugar, pressed
into an egg-cup and turned out as though from a
'shape'. I forget all the proceedings, but I do
remember that we always finished by dancing Sir
Roger de Coverley together, holding up our long
dresses and doing all the figures, and taking all the
parts of all the couples. One or other of us in these
games would be Mrs. Williams at the castle. How
we longed for a curled fringe!

Sometimes we played churches, when Susan was
always the organist and I the preacher, wearing one
of the boys' cricket shirts for a surplice. We were
also the entire congregation imitating the entry of all
our friends into their seats. But 'young ladies' was
played oftener than churches, the joys of earthly
hospitality evidently touching us more nearly than
the solemn rites of the church militant. Yet even
Cap'n would join us in a funeral.

8

TOYS AND BOOKS

My tale is done, there runs a mouse;
Time for bed, children.
One more page to finish this story
One more page to finish this
One more page to finish
One more page to
One more page
One more
One

—Once Upon a Time

WE had few toys. My most treasured possession for a long time was a hanging crystal from a chandelier which had been turned out of the parlour when my mother suddenly found herself hating chandeliers. Not only did the lustrous, heavy glass please me, but when I looked through certain planes of the crystal every common object was rainbow-edged. My first icicles were even more attractive. One cold spell, we had left water out in an old cup, because someone had said that in freezing it would expand and break the cup. It had not broken the cup, but the water had turned into a cloudy lump which we were looking at when Cap'n came dashing in to say there were icicles on Cap'n Math's shed. He

seized me by the hand and we tore off to see his
icicles before they had time to melt. Sure enough
there they were hanging from the galvanized roof—
pointed, clear, stiff, brittle water. We threw up
stones to break off some of these clear sticks of rock,
and we sucked them, making the dark pain come
at the back of our eyeballs, as it came when in
summer we were as thirsty as dogs, and drank cold
water too fast.

Susan used to tell me of a crystal ball she had
seen when she went to tea with Mrs. Morrison, wife
of the Scotch cowman at Caerhays, and otherwise
famous as a maker of scones which were three-
cornered, whereas our 'splits' were always round.
Mrs. Morrison's crystal, Susan said, would show
snowflakes falling if one turned it upside down. I
longed to see this wonder and when, at last, I went
to the Morrisons' to tea, I played with the crystal
ball, and played with it, instead of going out to try
and find pheasants' eggs with George Morrison.
Mrs. Morrison had other delightful objects such
as a thimblecase made out of the two halves of a
walnut. The halves were joined by a little hinge,
so that one could open and shut the walnut. A
coach and six might have driven out of it at any
minute.

My next favourite object was a little pair of
scales which Maurice gave me for one of my birth-
days. They were almost an exact replica of the scales

in Agnes's shop. The stand was black, the shaft and the beam were of brass and one did the weighing in little brass pans suspended by three chains from either end of the beam. There were real weights. I can feel my hands stripping the pennyworts of their 'rice', weighing it up, and twisting paper packets in Agnes's professional way for anyone who would buy of me. The golden maize grains which we gave the fowls were stock-in-trade when I played shops. I sold maize on ivy-leaves, and maize on pennyworts, or, for large orders, a whole handful of maize wrapped up in a dock-leaf.

Susan and I had dolls, dolls that would open and shut their eyes, and dolls that would squeak 'Mama' if pressed; nevertheless our favourite doll was a wooden stool dressed in various discarded baby-clothes, and christened in our wash-hand basin as a member of the Church of England. We baptized her Gwendoline. This doll with her bland-looking wooden forehead made me cast longing eyes at an advertisement of a very large doll which was appearing in various papers at the time. A picture of the doll, elegant and smiling, bore the legend beneath: 'Baby's clothes will now fit dolly'. No money was required for the doll; all one had to do was to send for some samples of cloths for cleaning silver, sell the cloths to obliging friends, send the money to the address stated and the doll would be the reward. All alone, for Susan despised it, I set about this commercial undertaking. I received the cloths, and in some confusion, sold them to my friends' parents. I sent the money up and, with eager expectation, watched for Jabez Gross, our postman. At last Jabez brought the reward, but I could not believe my eyes. It came in an envelope; it was nothing but a rag doll, a picture of a doll printed on calico to be cut out and stuffed. That doll, folded up like a tea-cloth, cost me a great deal of chaffing. Everybody knew.

I am not sure that the dolls we liked best of all were not the dolls Aunt Sarah showed us how to make out of poppies, single, scarlet, wild poppies. We would take a poppy on a stalk, bend back its lovely petals to make a skirt, tie a wisp of grass round to make a waist, stick a grass stalk through for arms, and let the black head of the poppy form the head of the doll. These dolls were like dancers standing gaily on one leg—fairy creatures. I do not know how we had the heart thus to spoil the poppy petals for we knew the poppies were alive. We would keep watch on the bursting buds to try to catch a poppy in the act of opening. We knew how the petals showed first crushed and crumpled from their packing in the bud; we knew how the sun ironed them out smooth and perfect; and yet we could spoil them without a pang. We tried to make scarlet dye from their petals, just as we tried to make scent from rose-petals, and from violets, just as we would bite the bottoms of the honeysuckle florets to taste the infinitesimal drop of nectar, or roughly uncurl the coppery-fringed bracken fingers, or hart's-tongue tips. One day I tore a whole sunlit host of honeysuckle growing on the bottom hedge of Furzy Brake. I jumped and climbed until I had pulled down the sprays that floated highest; I wanted them for my mother. But that day, when I had picked my great bunch, I knew I had spoilt something. Sometimes we would join in a passing craze for pressing flowers, or in a hunt for skeleton leaves; or we would press tutsan leaves, or boy's-love, or lemon verbena to keep between the leaves of our Bibles.

Not many of the things we played with were bought for us. I do not remember this as a hardship; Maurice does. He says he once eyed a little sailing boat in Sammy Warne's shop at St. Austell. He wanted it, and wanted it, and wanted it. Each time he went to St. Austell he went to gloat until, one day, it was gone. Some luckier boy than he had had it. He remembers quite distinctly saying to himself that he would give his children everything they asked for when he was grown up. Susan and I certainly wanted a doll's pram and were not given it; but then Ellen Sargent made us an incomparable doll's bed. Muslin curtains it had hanging from a circular canopy; and it had a real mattress and bedding, even to a bolster cloth and pillow-cases.

A sailing boat or a doll's pram might be with-held; but books never. Mr. Frederick Warne of St. Austell was our bookseller. His rather dark shop had shelves nearly to the ceiling; and I can see him standing on a ladder, his pencil stuck behind his ear, handing down to my father two little books bound in dark blue leather, the books were *Tom Brown's School Days* and Lamb's *Tales from Shakespeare*. Why the appearance of these books made so strong an impression on me I do not know. They were pocket editions on thin paper, seeming to be born for the parlour; yet they were to be on our own bedroom shelves. Schoolmasters had the seemly privilege of a good discount on books in those days and, in addition, there were children's windfalls in the shape of specimen copies.

Usually I cared little for the outsides of books. Like all my family I dived straight into the print. Reading came as naturally to us as eating; I believe if Nip and Tweed and Dart could have been pro-vided with print suitable to their minds they would have learned to read by contagion. Our range was wide. The other day I was in a lending library when a small boy arrived with three books to change for his mother. The librarian said, 'What does your mother want, sonny, two loves and a murder, or two murders and a love?' Our reading at the School House was not so lush, though it tended to be gory. My mother liked her gore tinged with history; I have seen her take a lurid cover from the back of a book and put on something more sober, so as to avoid being teased by my father. Her favourite books were romances, memoirs, and domestic novels. She read her favourites by Trollope about once a year. I have never seen anyone else read with such complete absorption, the tears cruising unnoticed down her cheeks in tales of disaster. She was tender-hearted, and pity runneth soon in gentle heart as Chaucer knew.

Although my father cared for books—he liked to buy, not borrow them—I would not call him a reader in the sense that my mother was a reader. He read with critical detachment; my mother with headlong abandon. He would leave any book to go out rabbiting in winter, or to enjoy the summer sun. My mother would be glued to the page until the climax was reached and passed. I have seen her with a great pile of mending by her side take a book as though drawn by an irresistible magnet. 'I'll just read a page or two first', she would murmur and in a moment she would be lost to the needle. There was time for reading when the lamp was lit, and the curtains were drawn, and the winter nights grew longer and longer. We played, too, but reading was the greatest resource. Only Susan liked making things. She did not like neat sewing any better than I, but she was wonderful at making pretty things with a light stitch here and there on this and that.

She liked reading too. I learnt to read, I imagine, by watching the words as Susan read aloud to me. Looking back it seems as though, at one minute I was being teased for not being able to read at all, and the next minute I could read anything in print.

Apart from nursery rhymes and picture books with such stories as Cinderella, Puss-in-Boots, and Red Riding Hood, the first story I vividly remember is 'So-fat and Mew-mew'. Susan would read me this little tale and we both adored it. It began: 'So-fat and Mew-mew were a little dog and cat. One day they made up their minds to run away.' The naughty creatures went through a pitiful series of adventures, but always brave, clever So-fat comforted and supported Mew-mew, and licked her paws when they were sore. At last, when our souls had been harrowed by the suffering of the pair, there came a turn in the story comparable to the moment when the Ancient Mariner sees again his church and hill and lighthouse top. Mew-mew suddenly recognized a gate or a hay-rick, or a friendly cock; and magically they were at home. 'They made up their minds never to run away again.'

Next came fairy tales. My father was generous in provision of these both in his family and school. One serious-minded Bible Christian remonstrated with him, saying that he was filling up the children's little noddles with what wasn' true and couldn' be true. Better fit the children read their Bibles than old lies. My father read him the Old Testament story of the trees who wanted a king; how they asked the olive and the olive said, 'Should I leave my fatness, wherewith by me they honour God and man, and go to be promoted over the trees?' My father said, 'Did the vine and the olive and the bramble really speak?' Mr. H. said it was different if it was in the Bible; but he did not complain any more.

We had a rich collection of fairy tales, but we tended to read the same ones over and over again. Generally speaking I liked Grimm better than Andersen, but there were a few of Andersen's I liked better than any Grimm. Andersen was in dark blue covers with gold on the back; Grimm was light blue and had plain covers. When I was tired of dominoes, or five-stones, or of making card pagodas, there was Andersen, ready to fall open at some well-worn page—*Little Claus and Big Claus*, *The Snow Queen*, *The Little Mermaid*, *Eliza and the Eleven Swans*, or *The Red Shoes*. I fancy Little Claus was my equivalent to Charlie Chaplin, the little funny poor chap getting the better of the rich, serious, bad big fellow. And Little Claus had a horse. He would shout when he had borrowed all Big Claus's beasts, 'Gee up, all my six horses! Gee up, all my six horses!' Gold was measured by the bushel; great blows were struck, and cunning tricks planned. Little Claus's horse was cracked on the head with a hatchet; Little Claus's old dead grandmother was cracked on the head with a hatchet. Little Claus made pretended magic by treading on his sack and making it squeak. It was fun to be in the loft watching with Little Claus while the farmer's wife gave roast meat and wine to the Sexton; more fun still when one heard the farmer arriving on his horse, and he and Little Claus went into the house and Little Claus conjured the hidden good things out of the oven, and the hidden Sexton out of the chest. 'What does your sack say now?' asked the farmer. Best fun of all was when Little Claus turned the tables entirely on Big Claus, enticed him into the sack, and flung him into the river to seek for shadow-cattle. No punishment of a villain was too vindictive for us.

The Little Mermaid with her red sun-garden under the sea, and her statue of the Prince, was likely to induce that curious feeling, impossible to explain and unpredictable, which we called feeling lonely. It was not fear, but a mood of desolateness. Fear stalked us in the wicked Marshes through which the Mermaid had to pass in order to reach the dwelling of the witch who gave her the burning drops to sprinkle on her fish's tail. But it was the end of the story which was likely to make one feel lonely. The elder sisters, their white arms linked, their hair shorn as a gift to the witch, brought a sharp knife that the Little Mermaid might plunge it into the heart of the Prince. He had not loved her and given her a human soul. If she killed the Prince she would return to her father's palace under the sea; otherwise she must become sea-foam. She went to look at the sleeping Prince, and she threw the knife far out to sea as the sun rose. I read this story so often and so intently that I seemed to swim in and out among the Sea King's treasures, and to ride the crests of the waves with the Little Mermaid as they lifted her high so that she could look into the ship in the storm and watch the Prince. When Johnny Hurrel took us out in his boat in summer, and we rowed near rocks rooted deep in purple water, and peered down into the depths at huge weeds swaying, and creatures gliding, the story of the Little Mermaid was not fabulous.

The places we knew provided settings for our stories. In the story of 'Eliza and the Eleven Swans' the little rock which the swans had to reach before sundown, when they were carrying Eliza over the sea, was a rock 'down Hemmick', with the sea all round it, and only just room for the brothers to stand on when they were changed into human form. The agony of suspense—would they reach the little rock in time—was renewed with each reading. In the same story the churchyard to which Eliza went to gather nettles to spin into flax, and make shirts for her brothers, was Gorran Churchyard. It was the dark, gloomy part, towards Cotna

Lane. Ghouls seated on the railed-in tombstones might well have stretched out horrible hands.

The Red Shoes was a story with a moral, but we never noticed that. 'Karen thought only of her red shoes', of those red shoes which she had secured by tricking the short-sighted old lady who had adopted her, and who would not have approved of red morocco shoes for church at all. It is when the old soldier says, 'But they are dancing shoes' that the horrible part of the story begins. For Karen is forced to go dancing over the world; through thorns and briars she danced; she danced until she was utterly weary and still the shoes would not let her rest. So she found the hangman's house and she said, 'Cut off my feet, cut off my feet'. And he cut them off and the little feet in the red shoes went dancing over the world by themselves. That hangman and the little dancing feet were more horrible than anything else I read.

We liked stories with detail. Part of the enchantment of *The Snow Queen* was the neighbourliness of the rooms in which Kay and Gerda lived, so close to each other that they could step out on to a common parapet and sit under the rose trees in the window-boxes. Those roses were as real to us as the roses in Cotna garden. And the snowflakes in the storied winter surpassed the real. No flakes in Gorran danced and veered and flew as thick and fast as the flakes in *The Snow Queen*. These were a poet's snowflakes and could be as large and as many as he chose. And the window panes could be as beautifully patterned by frost as he chose. And what a device it was of Kay and Gerda's to heat a copper ha'penny on the stove and press it against the pane to make a splendid peep-hole! I could feel my right eye squinting in readiness to look through that clear round hole in the frostiness. All the properties in the story were good. Kay's sled for example. If we could have had enough snow to go flying down hill on a sled we should have burst with exhilaration. All the other properties and people were endeared to us: the old woman's cottage and garden; the little robber maiden with her reindeer whose neck she tickled with her sharp knife; the Lapland woman and the Finland woman; the solemn cold palace of ice where Gerda kissed Kay and melted his frozen heart until he wept the little distorting bit of glass out of his eye. 'And they lived happy ever after.' 'Once upon a time.' Even the beginnings and endings of the tales were to a cherished pattern as my sister and I read them in the tree we called 'the wagon', or entwined together on a couch that had been Granfer's, and which we always called 'Granfer's couch'. The poetic essence of the Grimms' tales we read is in a lyric in George Peele's 'The Old Wives' Tale'. No other few words evoke so potently the stories in which ripe apple trees cry, 'Shake me! shake me!' and magic is natural:

Gently dip, but not too deep,
For fear thou make the golden beard to weep.
Fair maiden, white and red,
Comb me smooth, and stroke my head,
And thou shalt have some cockell-bread.
Gently dip, but not too deep,
For fear thou make the golden beard to weep.
Fair maid, white and red,
Comb me smooth, and stroke my head,
And every hair a sheaf shall be
And every sheaf a golden tree.

Cap'n had a large, heavy copy of the *Arabian Nights* bound in red which he would lend at a price. His too was a little green-backed book called *Froggy's Little Brother*. He would say, 'Very well, if you won't field you shan't have my Froggy tonight. Now see the mighty J.A.' And he would straddle with his bat like J. A. Cumberlidge, a friend of my father's, and a famous cricketer at Mount Charles. I cannot explain our attachment to Froggy. Froggy lived in a garret, swept a crossing, and brought up his little brother Benny on penny meat pies. He was very good and courageous, and I fancy Benny must have died, for it was a 'sad' book. So was *Little Meg's Children*. Perhaps she lived in a garret too. We wept over her; but garrets were romantic.

Oddly enough we did not weep over *Uncle Tom's Cabin*. We chiefly read about Aunt Chloe's Cabin—as desirable as a garret—the escape of Eliza with little Harry over the ice-floes; and the Topsy episodes. The escape of Eliza's husband, George, was a part we incorporated into various games. The slaver would chase George and the Quaker up our pile of sticks where there was one great tree-trunk leaning against the closet. George would say 'Are your pistols in order?' and he and the Quaker would get up to the topmost point of the tree-trunk. The slaver would shin up after them and the Quaker would say, 'Thee ist not wanted here, friend', and push him down. I thought for a long time that a Quaker was a fierce fighting chap, good for shoving.

When I was about nine Howard read me the first part of *The Swiss Family Robinson*. I would have given anything to be out in a storm on the sea, and in one of those lashed tubs with all the useful things which were to serve the family on the island. When the cattle and dogs were let loose from the wreck, and given a chance to swim behind the tubs, or rest paws or legs on them, it seemed to me better than Noah's Ark. For in addition to the animals and the tools there was Mamma's enchanted bag. Noah's wife had not thought of such a thing. It never occurred to me to jeer at the bag, nor indeed at the Robinson children. I fear I accepted Fritz, James, Ernest and little Francis in all good faith. I enjoyed the book up to the point where the boa constrictor swallowed the donkey. That did for me. I can see those waves of crushed donkey progressing through the inside of the boa constrictor yet; I used to read the book to myself until it neared that point, and stop. I turned over to the end, but never got the hang of it. I've an idea that my son Fritz—he was the hunter and sportsman of the family—found a girl called Jenny in a tree. I had no use for strange girls coming in to disrupt families. This disruption happened too often. Edward Beverley in *The Children of the New Forest* fell in love with a girl called Patience and the story went to pieces. What a good story it was when the Beverley children were still young— proud Edward and resourceful Humphry, and Alice and little Edith. I liked stalking deer with Edward, but even better I liked bringing in domestic creatures with Humphry. He got hold of ponies, and a heifer, and made a regular farm of it. A delightful life those children lived in that forest. Forest! The very word in the title ensured the success of the book.

The Swiss Family Robinson and *The Children of the New Forest* were in the boys' book-case. Here were stores of books which my brothers were now discarding and which I seized upon. Susan did not like adventures, but when we grew out of fairy-tales I read little else for some years. *Alice in Wonderland* I had at just the wrong age. I was too old and yet not old enough. I had looked forward to it enormously, for it was to come by post as a birthday present. It was coming from Warne's, and I was told what a lovely book it was. It came; I stayed away from school to read it, and I was sick with disappointment. I thought it silly. Not until I was grown up did I realize what my elders meant by praising the book to the skies as they did. 'How dreadfully savage!' said Alice, when told of the head-severing propensities of the queen. But I liked something really dreadfully savage. I could not appreciate 'It's a fine day, your majesty, quavered the Duchess', which was current as a saying in the family circle; and I did not see through the puns. The only thing I liked was the Cheshire Cat.

When I should have been delighting in Alice I was absorbed in such stories as *Cast up by the Sea*, *The Three Midshipmen*, *Through Fire and Through Water*, and *Snow Shoes and Canoes*. I cannot say how often I read these books. *Cast up by the Sea* had a Cornish setting, but it had a little of everything in it—smuggling, press-gang, shipwreck, desert island, a black boy, and savages. I cannot remember the course of the story at all, but I do remember a wicked old hag called Mother Lee who would mutter 'Luck comes from the south-west'. When she lit fires on the headlands to guide the smugglers in they would say, 'Mother Lee is trimming her lamps'. There was a fearful picture of her on the cover of the book all going up in flames. I fancy she caught herself afire in a storm when she was kindling false lights.

The Three Midshipmen were boys in the navy

at the time of the Napoleonic wars. I enjoyed their story so much that Maurice sent me for one birthday *The Three Lieutenants*, *The Three Captains* and *The Three Admirals* all bound up in one volume. But alas! my three daredevils grew less interesting as they advanced in their profession. An admiral's scope is more limited than a midshipman's for purposes of dashing narrative. The lower the rank the greater the flair for danger. In *Through Fire and Through Water* the boy was not even a midshipman; he was a powder monkey. Jack was his suitable name. He was nearly shot by highwaymen before he went to sea at all. He was driving over Salisbury Plain with Mr. Box the coxswain and others when a horseman galloped out of the night and shouted, 'Your money or your life'. Jack lunged at him with a carriage umbrella, but not before he felt his scalp creep. The shots went through his cap, but did not touch his head. Mr. Box said to him that night when they went to bed in a Portsmouth tavern, 'Say prayers, boy, don't mind me'. His other saying was, 'Hold tongue, boy, no sauce'. Once they got aboard the frigate—I had to have frigates in my stories—the narrative was a succession of fights. Then Jack rescued his Captain's daughter on a runaway horse at Valetta, and he was shipwrecked with Mr. Box and the surgeon in desert Africa. I remember the mirage. There was also a mirage in *The White Kangaroo*. Jack and Mr. Box and the

Surgeon were made slaves in Algiers. But Lord Exmouth bombarded Algiers and the slaves were released. I remember bits of Lord Exmouth's letter beginning, 'Lord Exmouth to the Dey of Algiers'. I was thrilled when someone told me Lord Exmouth was a Cornishman.

Marryat I liked, especially *Midshipman Easy*, *Peter Simple* and *Poor Jack*. Q's *Black Rock* was a prime favourite. Henty I never greatly cared for, though I read him. Ballantyne was better: 'A heavy hand was laid upon my shoulder; it was Bloody Bill'. There were few school stories, but one called *Tom, Dick, and Harry* I remember vividly. It came out either in *Chums* or the *Boy's Own Paper*, both of which journals we took. It began 'A shot! A bang! Silence!' and it had a rhymed letter in it. It had never occurred to me up to that moment that a letter could rhyme. The hero or rather the buffoon of the story—for he was always doing foolish things— was nicknamed Sara. On one occasion after he had got himself burnt in a fire, his mother had a tea-party for his friends to enliven his convalescence. One of them replied to the invitation in this astonishingly witty way:

> Dear Mrs. Jones I'll come to tea,
> At three o'clock you shall me see,
> I'm sorry Sara's been laid up
> And drinks his physic from a cup.
> And now, farewell, as great John Knox said
> Yours truly Samuel Wilberforce Coxhead.

Memory is a strange, fickle, undiscriminating jade. There is much lovely poetry I would gladly be able to recall; instead I have irretrievably fixed in my mind this idiotic fragment.

I read no girls' school stories. *Little Women* I did not read till much later. I could not be induced to begin a book with such a title as *Little Women*. I despised it. A girls' book I desired was a story of which the synopsis was given among the advertisements on the back of *From Fag to Monitor*. I read this synopsis again and again. I savoured the title— *For the Sake of a Friend*. When I asked for the book the others teased me so much that I hid my desire with shame; but I am sure that one reason why my first published books consisted of four girls' school stories was *For the Sake of a Friend*. I wrote in my age what I was unable to read in my youth.

I did not read much poetry—none to myself. Susan used to say 'Over hill, over dale', to me in bed. The only other poem I remember liking is 'Mazeppa':

> Bring forth the horse, the horse was brought;
> In truth he was a noble steed,
> A Tartar of the Ukraine breed
> Who looked as though the speed of thought
> Were in his limbs, but he was wild . . .

Dart was my Tartar of the Ukraine breed; if I could have met a few other wild horses and dashed in among them I should have been happy. But the only herd we ever chanced to meet was Barton cows.

Of all writers the one who held me entirely spell-bound was Scott. My brother Maurice introduced me to him when I was twelve or so. Maurice was home from London for a long vacation; he was working for an examination and did most of his reading on the cliffs above Portluney. We would bathe together. I, as though from Mamma's en-chanted bag, would produce a piece of cake or an apple; then we would go up on the cliffs among the kidney vetches and the bladder campions and read. No doubt Maurice told me a little about *Anne of Geierstein*, and gave me the book to keep my busy tongue still. I have forgotten most of the story, but I shall never forget the beginning—the moun-tains, and the mists, the two travellers, and Anne saving the younger traveller after he had crawled along the face of a terrific wall of mountain with a raging torrent beneath. I think Anne came skipping lightly from rock to rock and standing poised against the sky just after a mass of rock had slowly detached itself from under the young man and fallen with reverberating echoes into the abyss leaving him cold at heart but clinging to a tree. It went something like that. Grand stuff. I know after reading it that in all our balancing feats in the village—we were always balancing on top bars of gates or the school railing or tree branches—I was that young man with an abyss not only on one side, but on both; my progress a simple bee-line through space.

After *Anne of Geierstein* I read *Quentin Durward*. I chose it because Howard told me that Charles of Burgundy came into that too. He told me about Louis XI praying to the little figures on his hat, and about the astrologer who tricked Louis and saved his own life. I enjoyed reading that incident in the story. I cannot remember the order in which I read the rest of Scott, but I think I read all except *The Pirate*, *Tales of a Grandfather*, the poems, and the short stories. I liked my stories long, the longer the better. I would look regretfully at the thin number of pages remaining to be read in a grand book. *Tales of a Grandfather* had a title that repelled me; yet I was not put off by such titles as *The Antiquary* and *The Heart of Midlothian*. If any reader could, by an exercise of will, have made a character in a book obey his dictates I should have made Jeannie Deans tell a lie for Effie. I pretty nearly pushed her into it. But no, she would not. No doubt I skipped a great deal in the stories, especially the beginnings; and the Scotch words annoyed me. But I always gathered enough to follow the divagations of the unknown horseman or disguised maiden to the moment when expectation was generously satisfied. The Knight of the Leopard stood revealed as Kenneth of Scotland; the Black Knight was no

other than the Lion-heart himself. Di Vernon's
strange gallopings were made clear and Mary
Seaton and her twin brother ceased to plague Roland
Graham by their dual identity. I lived the story I
happened to be reading pretty nearly as intensely
as I lived my own life. 'What doest thou here in
Helen Macgregor's country?' I would shout to the
sea-gulls from what I considered some inaccessible
crag. I would be any character from the bow-
legged Smith to Fenella; from Alice Lee to Meg
Merrilies; from the Gaberlunzie to the Earl of
Montrose. It was nothing to me to be a flaming
Highland torch one minute and the Earl of Leicester
the next. What trap-doors I went down! What
rusty locks turned in their hinges behind me! What
panels slid open! What pictures moved in their
frames! Could the fleeing Prince Charles only have
had Dart and me in his service, he would soon have
put his foot on Cromwell's neck. What gallops I
had on secret missions! I wish I still needed only
a deserted chapel, a winding path, a friar in a cell,
a flagon of wine and a venison pasty to set me
wandering in the enchanted forests of romance.
But alas! Edith Plantagenet will no longer drop a
rose at my feet, and Saladin's scimitar is blunted.

Scott never frightened me; whereas I did not
read Dickens for years because of my early fear of
Quilp's malignancy. Part of the *Pickwick Papers*,
which Howard read aloud, was the only Dickens

given the chance to make me laugh when I was young. I suppose such characters as Andrew Fairservice were more within my humorous comprehension than the funny characters in Dickens. I remember a remark of Fairservice's about the weather and gardeners—that if there chanced to be a fine day Sunday would come along and lick it up. This struck me as most amusing. Sundays were always licking up our fine days. But Scott's necromancy left me free of fear; yet at the time when I was reading Scott I would play with fears. At Caerhays my father continued to take *The Western Morning News*, but Mr. Bellamy, our Rector, took *The Times*. The two papers were interchanged at night by the obliging medium of Anne. On winter evenings, running down the dark drive under the trees, I would play at shying at shadows, like Dart, for I was not really frightened. Sometimes the winds would be holding carnival in and out the great branches of the trees which moved in the darkness. If I put my arms round the trunk of a tree I could feel the life of the wind stirring even in it and in me. My evening world could be turbulent and eerie, but there were no fears such as must have haunted Mr. De la Mare's childhood. The occasion when my blood ran coldest was when William Smith went mad for love of Miss Blacket, and he came up to the School House, and he lifted my father clean off his feet.

9

VILLAGE SCHOOL

Walled in an hour,
Then with a shout
Out, out again,
To field and lane.

UNLIKE my elder brothers I did not want to go to school. Maurice and Howard, at four and three respectively, had embarrassed master by appearing in his big room as smutty as tinkers, one riding the poker and the other the fire-shovel. The two eluded my mother and invaded the school premises so often that at last they were formally placed on the register. Susan went to school when her time came, but left as early as possible and, except for music, for which she went to St. Austell, finished her education at home. The result was lovely—I have met only a few other people so little injured by formal education.

I could not be induced to go to school at all as an 'infant'. I learned to read at home by no method; most of the methods are more complicated than the end they serve. I also learned to cook; I dearly loved the kitchen. My world did not seem furnished until somebody had lighted the kitchen fire—it was Cap'n's job for a good many years. No wonder the hearth-fire has become a symbol. The dead ashes would be taken away and, all bright and clean, the flames would shoot up the chimney, while Cap'n watched with a smut on his nose. We had an old-fashioned Cornish stove. The fire could be either 'open' or 'turned down' to heat the oven. In the early morning it was open. We had breakfast in the kitchen.

When the others had all gone off to school I entered into my kingdom of garden, lane, thorn tree, trap-house, wood-pile, wash-house and kitchen. The kitchen was not a little modern cooking labora-tory with every inch of space utilized, and everything having to be in its place because there is no room for it anywhere else. It was the sunniest room in the house; it was biggish; it had a fire, a hearth-rug, an armchair, other chairs, a settle, a solid table with drawers, pretty window-curtains, a picture of Ellen Terry on the wall, and a blue stone floor. It was the hub of the house as the kitchen of a little house should be. Above all it was warm. No woman would want to hurry out of it.

My mother would first make herself a fresh cup of tea and look at *The Western Morning News* which my father had monopolized during breakfast. She never read a book in the morning. Even when we were grown up and able to provide an easier life for her, she told me she never read in the mornings without a guilty feeling. She could reprove me in those later days for the way I skipped through the house-work and say my only merit was dispatch. She did not aim at dispatch. She had the inestimable gift of conferring grace and comfort on a house. We would call to her to be reassured she was there—'mother'—almost before we opened the door.

Each day had a different routine and a different smell. Monday was washing day with the copper fire burning in the wash-house. Various people washed for us in my childhood, Mrs. Clarke is my chief memory, an oldish woman with a little bun of silvery hair at the back, and hands crinkled with washing. There would be three heavy wooden trays mounted on stocks in the wash-house, one for the first water, one for the second water and one for the blue. White clothes would go through the second water into the copper and out of the copper into the blue. In the copper which was filled from the wash-house pump the water would be bubbling and steaming. The wash-house was soon full of steam. Mrs. Clarke could usually be persuaded to give me some water and soap and even, when in a good humour, some blue and some starch. I did my washing in the dipper, and when weary of washing I blew bubbles. Like most Cornish women Mrs. Clarke enjoyed having children about. I dearly liked hanging up the clothes. The skirts and the knickers and the pillow-cases would billow out and dance in the wind. Wet Mondays were calamities.

The modern airing cupboard in little houses is an enormous boon. We had no airing cupboard, and we all hated the business of drying off in the wash-house and kitchen. It must be remembered that there was no laundry service at all. We were ten miles from the nearest laundry. Even the sheets and blankets were washed at home. I am all for modern laundries. But the clothes we washed at home and dried on the line hoisted high above the three-cornered piece were wonderfully fresh and sweet. Tuesday was ironing and mangling day. No form of labour is more immediately rewarding than ironing, the rough becomes smooth as though with pleasure, and it is delightful to put on clean freshly ironed clothes. In those days to be entrusted with the handkerchiefs to iron was a treat. Now I haven't patience to iron anything. The secret of a happy life is to do the right things at the right age. Very little girls usually like helping to keep house. It is a form of play. A very small niece of mine enveloped in an apron, and washing up the tea-things while I dried them, sprinkled some Vim into her sink when the job was completed and said gravely, 'I always like to vim me sink'. In a few years' time to vim the sink will be merely a tiresome necessity instead of a delightful promotion to grown-up responsibility.

Wednesday and Thursday were ordinary days— bedrooms were cleaned on Wednesdays, the downstair rooms on Thursdays. I never did like the smell of furniture polish; I made myself scarce on these days and early made up my mind I did not want a house of my own. But on Friday mornings I knelt on the settle with my elbows on the table alert and eager. Baking day! Mr. Hicks the baker brought our bread from Mevagissey, but my mother made the yeasty buns and cake. Cooking as an occupation does not pall. As we were a big family my mother could play with really satisfying quantities of flour, white flour in a deep earthenware pan, yellow without and white within. Flour is a particularly well-named substance. To plunge one's arms into flour right up to the elbow—how much better than the finest sand or the most rich smooth mud! Then there would be a little salt, the fat to rub in, currants or sultanas to clean, lemon peel to cut up, sugar to add to the mixture, and a little crater dug in the floury mountain to put the yeast in. The yeast in milk, with a lump of sugar, would have been in a basin working overnight. Sometimes there was saffron rich in colour. When all the ingredients were in, the cake was wetted up, kneaded, and left to rise in a pan with a piece of clean blanket over it by the warm hearth. The rising always seemed miraculous, as indeed it was. The solid dough would rise and rise until it was ready to overflow the pan. When it was really plumb, or plimb—the spongy mass would be divided into the greased cake tins and in addition there would be a sheet of buns (knubbies) new for tea. Cake was not cut new, though sometimes when it came out of the tins, cleft, browned and crisp, I was given a hot crusty bit. Sometimes too I had a special bun which I had patted into shape myself; or if 'we' were making pasties—a little pasty. I could crimp a pasty with anyone when I was seven, and I have never lost the art. Another thing we made was yeasty splits. Yeasty splits with jam and cream! How foolish man is so to behave as to reduce his eating to bread-and-marge. My mother would have been horrified at the idea of margarine. We had butter from Agnes's, a half-pound at a time, yellow, rich and flaky, printed with a cow. Different farms had different prints. These prints ensured a standard of excellence. A good farmer's wife would be ashamed of bad butter under her ensign. One print which I liked very much, I think it was Tregerrick print, had a device in ears of wheat. A half-pound of butter, neat, upstanding, printed and placed on a lordly dish was common. 'There is enough for all', as Mrs. Ramsay might have said. But we did not, as children, have butter and jam; butter or jam was the rule. We could, however, have a piece of each at the same time and make a sandwich.

I was very loath to quit my homely pleasures for school, but at last I 'stood in lines' with the others in the playground. Of the first day I remember nothing; the picture in my mind of early school days is composite. I know I was small for my age, wiry and untiring; and that I wore a kilt and top, with an anchor worked in red on the sleeve, and a pinny to preserve my kilt from ill usage. My straight hair was parted at the side and tied on top with a ribbon, or it was combed back and worn with a ribbon like Alice.

The bell and the whistle were fun. Often we would play as far away from the school as possible; bell made us run towards school, whistle made us tear. I liked to play with May Gross and Francie Spears down Crooked Lane on a stile leading to Nicholls' Fields, or on a stone-heap down the same lane. This stone heap was perfect for playing 'mothers', as it afforded us material to build a fire-place in the sort of little house we made. The playground could just be reached if we waited for the bell at Nicholls' stile. In the girls' playground we stood in lines according to 'standards' or, on wet days, we played 'more sacks' in the lobby, until authority intervened. Then, to a tune on the piano, we marched, the girls by their door, and the boys by theirs, into the big room. On the boarded floor the boys in their hobnails made a sound like the trump of doom.

In the mornings we began with prayers and a well-sung hymn. I don't think any of us were in any doubt as to what we were supposed to be engaged in; whereas a little boy I know who went to a

village school recently, and whose mind had been
kept by his parents unprejudiced in the matter of
the gods, reported on the first day that they had
begun school with a funny game called 'Shut eye'.
The same child re-told the story of Adam and Eve
to his little sister. 'And Dod said, "Now don't you
touch that apple tree". And', very dramatically,
'they did. And Dod tame into the garden, and they
hided away, and Dod said, "You tum out of that".
And they tame out. And Dod said, "Now you do
out of this". And they went out and'—long pause—
'they had ice-cream each'.

We had scripture every day immediately after
prayers and I enjoyed it. For a child to be early
absorbed in figurative writing seems to me an
enormous advantage; and then there were the puzzles
of conduct. 'Was Balaam a good man?' my father
asked once after we had read the story. I said no
in decided tones. Had he not beaten his donkey?
But Balaam, it seemed, was a good man. It was
years before I realized that he was a man of vision.
Jacob, again, whom I detested, whereas I was ready
to weep for Esau when he said, 'Bless me, even
me also, O my father'. Why was Jacob chosen and
Esau rejected? Apart from the quality of the stories
the discussions which arose made us think. We
were engaged, in a simple way, on the proper study
of mankind. And the drama was of the violent
kind which children will have in some form or other.

I can see in my mind's eye two boys in Caerhays school enacting impromptu Elijah and Ahab. 'Art thou he that troubleth Israel?' 'I have not troubled Israel; but thou, and thy father's house, in that ye have forsaken the commandments of the Lord, and thou hast followed Baalim.'

I enjoyed scripture, but sums were another matter. I did not like sums. I could see through the problems, but made mistakes in working out. Quick and inaccurate was the verdict. And whereas my friends' sums would look beautifully neat mine, try as I might, would be smudged and blotted. The ink-pot had a devil. It was the same with writing. How glorious it was to have a new exercise book, and how careful one would be on the first page! Then the inevitable 'crossing out' and the quick deterioration in the spidery hand. Some of my friends never made a mistake. All was fair, and a delight to the eye. My father was not severe over my tattered script but he was severe with my flowers of speech. I still remember my mortification when I, having written about the lambs 'frisking in the verdant pasture lands', was told, 'playing in the green fields, Anne, playing in the green fields'. An excellent lesson in English. But though mortified in spirit I continued my floral tributes; I never could resist a word. The pleasure in using it was keener than the pang of the snub.

The subject I liked best of all was history—beginning with the stories I read before I went to school, with reprehensible instruction in partisanship from my brother. In the book I had at home was a picture of the Roman soldier of 55 B.C. or was it 54 B.C. dashing into the water with his Eagle, and calling the others to follow him. I showed this hero of my heart to Cap'n so that he too might admire. Cap'n said, 'But he isn't on our side', and pointing to the Britons on the cliffs, poor uncouth heathen with great rocks ready to heave at the handsome invaders, he said, 'Those are our chaps'. I was dumbfounded. I said I didn't want to belong to that lot, and I wasn't going to believe it. Cap'n said to my father, 'Aren't we Celts?' My father, who was reading, said absently, 'Yes, the Cornish are more or less Celtic'. Cap'n said, 'There you are, Anne, so are those Britons Celts. It's all the same. That one (pointing to the most ferocious-looking Briton) might have been your great, great, great, great, great grand-father. I dare say he was'. It was most disturbing. I knew all about sticking up for my own side, and I fancy I really tried to transfer my affection to those Britons. So my historical sense was perverted by false patriotism at the very start! I wonder what little girls make nowadays of their scientific and pasteurized Histories. I expect their big brothers defeat the authors' laudable intents somehow.

In my first history books I merely enjoyed the drama of the various stories and, when I had got over the shock at the primitive appearance of my earliest forebears, the grandeur of being English. But the books had the advantage of initiating a permanent taste for history. And after all one advances. One does not remain a gazer at bad pictures of Britons on the cliffs and of Becket being hewn down at the altar. 'Will no man rid me of this turbulent priest?' What! I do hope it isn't all omitted from the new history books.

Geography I liked chiefly for the names. Other people made lovely maps which I wistfully envied. 'And don't 'ee make the coast-line too thick or you'll make smudges'. My father heard one of his pupil-teachers giving a class this advice in good broad Cornish. My coast-lines were always too thick, I suppose, for there were always smudges. Nevertheless hope sprang eternal. I could see the perfect map which I should one day draw. In the meantime I browned the mountains, greened the valleys, blacked the rivers, put a hint of blue round my coastline with a fish or two for fun, and printed in the names with a mapping pen. For some reason this fine pen-nib seemed immensely grand. I did not only maps I was supposed to do, but other maps from the boys' atlas. India and South America were my favourites. I liked Tierra del Fuego, and the river Bramaputra.

I think we worked harder in school than children do now. But the hours were short. My father did not like long hours himself. The tell-tale bell would often reveal to the village that he was giving the children a good long play-time. 'Master is reading the cricket news I s'pose'. But once in school he worked hard and so did the children. There was no idea that a pupil with a slow mind and disinclination for books could be allowed to do the practical work he excelled in and grow up illiterate. My father did not profess to teach boys to farm or give their work a 'rural bias'; but he did teach them so that they could keep their accounts when they had become successful farmers, have some enjoyment from reading, know something of the world and its history, and write a decent letter. A contemporary of mine at Gorran school, now one of the most knowledgeable men with sheep in the west country, told me that he'd been a dunce at 'problems', and hated to try until my father played a game of draughts with him and said, 'The same faculties that make you play a good game of draughts, John, could make you work out problems on paper'. John set to work with fresh heart. My father acted constantly on the assumption that a child's power of growth is in himself; he nurtured the germinal spirit; once a child 'had a mind to it' he knew that half the battle was won.

He was pretty free to teach as he liked by the time

I went to school. This freedom is a necessity. Schools not too big with good masters and mistresses free to help the individual children, and not cluttered up with secretarial work, should be the English pattern. Not schools all alike but rich and varied; our education had better remain too haphazard than too straightly planned. The schoolmasters of my father's day emancipated themselves from the Code and the grand parade of the annual examination; schoolmasters today need to emancipate themselves from the encroachment of directors, and from the army of planners, organizers and testers. A child is more than the sum of his analysed parts. He is a spirit and incalculable. He needs someone with faith in him. Surprise visits from His Majesty's Inspectors were paid in my day. Relations between Inspectors and inspected (the relation is that of Capital and small letters still) have become increasingly cordial as the 'I spy' attitude has declined, and it is of some benefit to the schools to be in contact with an outside mind. But inspect is a difficult word for a difficult art. I doubt whether inspection serves any very great purpose. Lazy teachers use their wits and dodge, and in any case a lazy schoolmaster does less harm than a ruthlessly ambitious and competitive one. He may even by some chance raise up a demon of endeavour in a boy. It would be better to spend the money on sabbatical years for teachers, sending them hither and thither round the world looking at things—not necessarily schools. The trouble with all schools is the stuffiness which tends upon their state. All teachers teach too long. The best schools in appearance can be the deadest. Life has a way of being inimical to that neat organization which appeals to inspectors. Plans! Records! Schemes! All so much easier to inspect than the living, growing Tommy and Alice, playing noughts and crosses under the desks. Children must indeed, like seeds, develop in the dark. How little count is taken of the individual force of soul working unseen to make each child into its utterly original unique self, enjoying its own felicity. Children are too often conceived of as passive, something to be manipulated, a danger accentuated in our age of frenzied planning. I hate the words 'creaming' and 'streams' and 'intelligence quotient'.

The swiftest improvement in elementary education would result from a determined effort to be rid of under-staffing. 'I will drain him dry as hay' I sometimes murmur when I see young teachers with their vitality being sapped by impossibly large classes and multitudinous duties. Given a really well-staffed school much work with 'youth' now being done by unattached youth-leaders and W.E.A. lecturers could be undertaken, and the whole venture co-ordinated. The germ of such an idea was in the old village school. In his younger days my father, in addition to teaching the older children in his school, taught two or three pupil teachers to what was the equivalent of the school certificate examination. He had a large night school for grown-ups. The first string band I ever heard, and it fiddled me off my head, was Sammy Rowe's at a night-school concert. Much that W.E.A. lecturer now does my father did. He also ran the cricket club and so forth. He worked too hard. But his work was varied and interesting and kept his own reading alive. Above all it was voluntary. The school was vital to the whole village and not merely to the young children. With a full-time and visiting adequate staff the work would not be too hard and the village school would regain significance in the community. A first-class schoolmaster living in a village is very different from a W.E.A. lecturer visiting it. The trouble has always been the effort made to staff cheaply.

The worst features of Gorran school were that the fires were covered up in great ugly black stoves, and that the windows were too high to look out of. There was only the sky to be seen. The best feature was that we were soon out of school, and that once out we had absolute liberty, with no supervision, no homework, and no meddling with what we chose to do with our own darling time. Lessons over, we played, with intoxicated zest, the game which happened to be in season. We had a grand succession of games, a ritual recurrence. Why a certain game should begin at a certain time I do not know, but some fine day conkers would be out and marbles would be in, or skipping-ropes and hoops would make an appearance, and hippety-beds be deserted. While a certain game was in season we played it with passion; then, for no apparent reason, we were all playing something else. Not all games corresponded to the weather. Marbles, for example, was not, as one would have expected, a warm weather game. No; boys blue with the cold would be playing knuckle under, and fingering their glass alleys. I never had skill in marbles, but I dearly loved Cap'n's glass alleys, and even his coloured ordinary marbles which he carried in a little bag tied with a running noose. Boys swopped marbles and won them from each other with a Shylockian air.

Girls would watch the boys play marbles, and back their champions, and sometimes play themselves. But it was not a girls' game. There was considerable distinction between boys' and girls' games. Boys never had skipping ropes; whereas we girls played 'All in together this frosty weather' for hours. Our hoops were different. Girls had wooden hoops and sticks; boys had iron hoops with iron crooks. Cap'n (if in a good temper) would lend me his iron hoop. Iron was associated with boys. In a sense they were shod with iron, for most of them wore hob-nails in their boots, and could strike

fire from the road flints as Dart could. I was ambitious for a pair of hob-nailed boots, and tried to
persuade John Parnel to put some hobs in when my
shoes were mended. The nearest he would come
to it was 'boot protectors'—little iron lozenges
cunningly shaped. I can remember, as if it were
yesterday, my joy in these protectors. When old
John Parnel handed my shoes with the protectors
in he said, 'There, my handsome, now you'll make
the stones bled'. Both boys and girls played
'Horses'. Boys would not often join in ring games,
but in summer the girls played a great variety
of these, and a few like 'The wind and the wind
and the wind blows high' were played in winter.
Other ring games I remember are, 'Walking round
the Village', 'Poor Sally sits a-weeping', 'Twos
and Threes'. A good many guessing games had a
formula. 'Here come I Lady Queen Anne' was
one. In summer I wonder how much time we spent
with meadow grasses playing 'Tinker, Tailor', or
in the lanes idling the hours with 'Even ash in
my hand'?

There were little game-cycles within the big
cycles, and some games like Edie Mop and Tig and
Puss in the Corner were, like gorse-flowers, in
season all the year round. A game called 'Old Man
Smack' which my mother told me should properly
be, 'Home Last, Smack!' could be counted on at
any old time of the year to be the rage for two or

three days at a time. In this one person as old man stood in the middle of the playground, and all the other people were in two 'Homes' on each side of the playground. The game was to run across from one home to the other and not be caught. If caught one joined the old man in the middle. All the caught people joined hands until to get through these rovers without being caught was a desperate venture. One had to be not merely touched, but absolutely captured; so one could tear along leaving any loose pieces of clothing in the hands of the enemy. It was a regular berserk game for the last two or three in the homes. The last person to be caught became 'old man' in the next game. A game similar to 'Old Man Smack' was 'Fire the Blazes'. We played a variety of this game after school over the fields when, as Fire, I used to chase the Gorran Haven children down to Rice or Cooks.

We spoke broad Cornish in the playground. Long may it continue. I can still speak it—not the Cornish language but the Cornish dialect—with anybody; and the only way to acquire it perfectly is in childhood. As far as I can hear in Cornwall the children seem to be keeping it going in spite of the attacks of the pedantic, and the zeal of the standardizers, and the anxieties of the too-class-conscious. I was with a friend the other day whose little boy is at a village school in Cornwall. As we were passing the playground she said to another boy, who sat on the wall, 'Denzil, will you tell Martin his mother wants him?' The shout went ringing across the playground, 'Curly, yer ma is holl'in'.

The only piece of apparatus we had for games was a stand with holes in the sides drilled by my father with a red-hot poker. Into these holes we stuck pegs. We then stretched a rope across resting on the pegs and played 'higher and higher'. I delighted in jumping. Jumping, sliding and riding induced a kind of physical beatitude. I wish I could have learned to skate as a child. We never had ice enough. But for brief periods we would be able to make excellent slides in the playground. We watered them to make them freeze on light snow. Then we played 'Keep the kettle boiling'. When I first read of Mr. Pickwick on the ice I knew he was a friend of mine, and that impression has continued.

In looking back at the play with which we sped the hours at Gorran I notice its freedom from anxiety. It was fun to jump highest in 'higher and higher', but it did not matter. Next day someone else might jump highest. No one kept a score; no game was competitive beyond the moment; play is no longer play if it serves some end other than that contained in itself. We did not play for our school, or our team, we just played; there was no responsibility except that demanded by the game itself; and so no dividing of the energies, no splitting of the person. The game demanded a kind of integrity; we were intent.

And these games were in some sort creative, never taught except by other children, and little interfered with or encouraged. Encouragement kills play. Hockey, which I greatly enjoyed in after years, is not play in the sense that our games at Gorran school were play. In *Family Reunion* T. S. Eliot makes a character say, 'We never had time to invent our own enjoyments'. It seemed to me to throw a flood of light on the characters he was depicting. I was interested to find when reading a life of Sir Humphry Davy, that Cornish education in his day left as much freedom for wandering by cliff and field as in my own. Sir Humphry said he enjoyed much idleness and he praised it. He said he believed he owed more to it than to the formal education he received at Penzance and Truro. He wrote, 'I consider it fortunate I was left much to myself as a child and put upon no particular plan of study. What I am, I made myself'. He left a hundred pounds, the interest of which was to be given to the pupils of his old school at Penzance, not on condition that they were meritorious and hard-working, but on condition that they were given a whole holiday on Sir Humphry's birthday. Do Penzance children get that holiday? Are holidays becoming suspect in that 'smooth and asphalt land' to which so many of our country children—even our babies—are now 'conveyed' by bus?

10

CAERHAYS

Silver and gold and jewels bright
Here are spread for your delight;

The raindrops on the birch your gems,
Your red-gold in the bracken stems;

Your silver in the festival
Shining of the sudden pool;

Poor as naked worm you fare
Who are to such vast riches heir,

A millioneth part you could not hold
Should you seek to grasp your gold.

Open heart and open eye
And all are yours for passing by.

—Bend in the Road

WE went to live at Caerhays when I was ten. As the distance from Gorran to Caerhays was only three miles our furniture was taken over in Caerhays Barton wagons. It was a wet and windy day; the tarpaulins flapped and the horses smoked; the beds got soaked and my mother said she would never change houses again. A saying we kept up for many years was spoken by one of our helpers, as our furniture, top-heavy and perilous, swayed on a wagon: 'Howard, is there room up there for the commoade?'

The School House at Caerhays was not joined to the school. It stood alone not far from the church, neat and new and too near the road for its height, like a top-heavy rick. Its situation was less windy than the Gorran house, but no one could call it sheltered. The red and pink roses which the Squire had had planted to climb up it never had quiet to climb. They would get a little way and the wind would take them; they flowered, but they flowered low.

Although it was a smaller house than school house Gorran, it had four bedrooms; and as even my youngest brother was now to be away from home except on Sundays, Susan and I moved into a bedroom each, Susan with rejoicing, I with reluctance. Our pink knotted nightdress-cases, lined with silk, no longer rested companionably on the same white counterpane. If one of us forgot to say her prayers we no longer lay in the bed's growing snugth discussing whether God wouldn't be just as pleased with our prayers if we said them where we lay as if we got out and knelt down in the cold to say them. At first I merely pretended to like the idea of separate rooms, but soon I came to value a sanctum all my own more than anything else in the house. I set up a bookcase with all the boys' discarded books in it.

We moved to Caerhays in the stormy beginning of Holy Week. By Good Friday the weather had changed to fine. After church we saw the various Caerhays men in their gardens teeling their taties, an established Caerhays custom. There they were— old Alfred Snell, crippled with rheumatism, but still gardening; Jim Beard, whom I always see in my mind's eye sitting on the shaft of his cart in the rain with a bag over his shoulders. Once we took his horse out of the harrow and he went right across the field without noticing. He would shout to me, meeting me wet through on a wild day, 'Good grawin' weather!' John Blandford was a game-keeper; but he was also one of the most assured and tidy gardeners in the place. His garden would all be 'in' before anybody else's, and his onions would come up in the most orderly rows. No lettuce, carrot, parsnip or shallot ventured out of line with John Blandford. In the right season the begonias and chrysanthemums in his front garden were a splendid spectacle—bronze chrysanthemums with gold-backed petals; and curled beauties of a colour between dandelion and furze. His double daisies were doubly double; his stocks extra-scented; his pansies pansier than ours. He had a growing family of children who became my friends. Mrs. Blandford always made tartlets on Saturdays for Sunday tea, and sheets of 'nubbies' which stuck together in the baking as they expanded in their lightness. She would break a bun off the regiment for us. Dorset people, the Blandfords were originally, but well worthy of their adoption in Cornwall.

Gardens were more thought on at Caerhays than at Gorran. The Sargents and the Martins at the Hovel had gardens never without bloom. A monthly rose bush in the Sargents' garden was one I particularly loved. Garden scents rather than wild scents lingered round Caerhays—lilies of the valley by the Martins' gate; moss-roses by the Sargents' gooseberry bushes; sweet violets or heliotrope under the Blandfords' wall; mignonette on either side of our own path; great tea roses over the Rectory veranda. All the land was more intensively cultivated than at Gorran; garden flowers grew even outside the gardens, but they were almost wild garden flowers, fragrant. The roses were not composed, scentless images, but full of nature, having the virtue of roses. Trees were heavier with leaves, birds' song riper—the coo of pigeons at the Hovel, the evening sermons of rooks as one went up Portluney hill from the beach. No Gorran birds cooed or preached. Lark was the Gorran bird.

I knew on the first Good Friday that Caerhays was all right—though not quite as good as Gorran. We walked to Portholland in sunshine. Celandines were sparkling. We went down through the sycamore avenue, half way up Barton Hill, over a stile on the right, and through a field called House Close.

Then we went down a steep field called Furzy Brake. Furzy Brake led to Stony Hill, from the top of which we could look down on Portholland, with its sea brimming full and bright. I knew I should be happy. We went along Barns Hills to see Dart. He was happy too, happier than he had been in Will Richards's field down Crooked Lane.

Caerhays was a hamlet rather than a village. A Church, seven cottages, a school, school house, a village Institute and the Rectory gate made up the whole of it. The Rectory itself was out of sight down a weedy drive, a rectory more beautifully situated than any other rectory I have seen; and most rectories and vicarages were built before houses defaced the sky-line. Mr. Bellamy lived in it, a bachelor parson very different from the saintly Mr. Martin, and quite different from old Mr. Sowel. Old Mr. Sowel was Cornish himself, and the only one who was ever called the passun. There was no passun's wife either at Gorran or Caerhays in my up-growing. Perhaps that is why relations between school house and rectory were so cordial. We loved Mr. Bellamy, a courtly person, not unworldly, an excellent preacher and Churchman. But he introduced a new element. It was from him I first heard the word protestant as a term of contempt. He disliked the Jubilate and would not have it. He called it 'that Protestant thing'. The Rectory was two fields away from the Hovel where the

Sargents and Martins lived. In addition there were
three houses at Pound, and a big old home-farm
called the Barton where the Kneebones lived, and
where I have shared so many delectable meals that
it amazes me my body does not show the better
for it. I always think of Mr. Kneebone as the
modern equivalent to Chaucer's Franklyn, and who
can say better than that? Down the drive was the
Castle itself, and there were a few outlying farms—
Polgrain, Little Polgrain, Polmenna, Tubsmill,
Trelucky, Treberrick and Polsue. Trevilveth must
have been in Veryan parish, I think. In Caerhays
itself there was no chapel. The little chapels were
in Portholland and West Portholland. Harsh words
have been said about the personal appearance of
the Cornish chapels. Some of the pretentious ones
are ugly. But some of the plain little ones in the
hamlets, and especially those on remote carns, have
something of the same appeal as beehive huts among
the furze and the bracken and giant outcrops of
granite. They touch us by their humanity. 'Where
you do worship 'tis your life almost' an elderly
woman said to me when Pentewan chapel was
bombed. Now the chapels are losing their strength;
but the study of the Bible which they encouraged
provided Cornish people with dignity of speech,
and a preoccupation with questions not paltry. ''Tis
a bitter cup she've got to drink out of' I have heard
of a person in grief; or 'It was a high dawn' of a

red sunrise, as though the rising of the sun were a splendid ritual. It is easy to poke fun at dressing up in Sunday clo'. I once perpetrated some verses which I called The Land of Sunday Clo':

> We never see the piskies,
> In mowy or in barn;
> We never catch the spriggans guarding
> Gold upon the Carn;
> But one enchanted land we know,
> It is the Land of Sunday Clo'.
>
> We wake up in the morning,
> And wash and brush our hair,
> We put on nice clean underthings
> That have been put to air.
> Then out of our rare front door we go
> Into the Land of Sunday Clo'.
>
> And soon a man may see us
> Walking in the street;
> With Sunday hats upon our heads
> And Sunday shoes on feet;
> We go to serve the God we know:
> Lord of the Land of Sunday Clo'.

Luckily He was not Lord only of the black suit and the best hat. I have often wondered what Cornwall would have been like if we had become predominantly Quaker instead of predominantly Wesleyan. One would have thought that with our make up we should have chosen either symbol and ritual at their richest, or extreme plainness. Instead we chose the communal halleluia! I believe it was because we liked singing hymns; or because we are emotional and inventive rather than artistic; we liked to give Billy Bray a chance to say his say in the pulpit as well as the Passun. Had we been Quakers our Meeting houses might have been the fit complement in appearance to our churches. I shall never forget coming upon the little Friends' Meeting House called 'Come to Good'. It was in spring, recently, when I was bicycling in Cornwall. Between Feock and Falmouth I came upon a building of extreme simplicity, with thick whitewashed walls, three inset latticed windows, and a roof with projecting eaves in brown rich thatch. At one end was a thatched lean-to supported by posts. The lean-to had straw on the floor. This straw and the ivy-grown mounting-block made me feel that a seventeenth-century group of Quakers might arrive at any moment and take exception to so carnally minded a sister as I. The trees were not in leaf; only budding. There were deep-rooted clusters of primroses with long stems in the hedges; hart's-tongue and lacy ferns were unfolding from the dead; late celandines glittered; cuckoo pints and blue speedwell. Bluebell leaves everywhere gave promise of the next flowery session. The window shutters were grey, and inside the Meeting house were benches of plain wood. There was a single seat where the altar would be in a church. Nothing was faked or concealed or decorated. I had come right across Cornwall from

Perranporth, where the sound of gun-practice was heard, and soldiers were standing to be moved like draughts on a draught-board. Here on the contrary was quiet; half dissolved in air and light, one might come to know the practice of the presence of God, and reach that Peace which passeth all understanding.

Our Wesleyan and Bible Christian chapels have not the quiet of 'Come to Good', but they have for their members the human friendliness of communion and singing. The Quakers valued silence; Cornish people eloquence. 'Did a preach un or did a read un?' will still be asked of a sermon. 'And if a didn' preach un, with no note in his hand mind you, he idn' up to much though he may be a nice chap enough and know the Word.'

Both Portholland and West Portholland had chapels; but sad to say I never once went to a service in either. To me Portholland suggests Mrs. Johns's shop, place of my frequent pilgrimage while we lived at Caerhays. Caerhays and Gorran people ordered their fundamental stores from Mr. Box at St. Austell. He sent a clerk round for orders once a month; and the goods ordered were delivered once a month by a horse van driven by an old wizened chap called Isaac. One Christmas Eve at Caerhays, when we were expecting Isaac to deliver the Christmas goods, he did not come. We were in consternation. Wherever is that old Isaac got to? Evening fell; the lamps were lit, and still no Isaac.

Eleven o'clock and we went to bed; and no Isaac. At about one o'clock the village was awakened, and Isaac stumbled in at the various doors with the customary wooden boxful of goods. So many people had 'treated' Isaac in their kitchens, it being Christmas Eve, that he had been overtaken by darkness, gone to sleep, and lost his way coming up the drive. He had got down to Noah's Ark, where his horse began to enter the water of the pond, and only saved himself and Isaac by his good horse-sense. Howard, who was home for the Christmas holiday, began composing with me a story about this adventure of Isaac's. It began 'It was snowing heavily. An old man ploughed his way . . .'

When my mother forgot to order anything from Box, Anne had to 'run down to Portholland for it'. In summer I could both shop and bathe. Portholland was a good safe bathing beach—too safe. Unless the tide was right for diving in from the side rocks, it meant a long wade through shallow water. Because of the sea-wall, and a kind of bastion behind which ran the public road, spring tides and rough seas were spectacular at Portholland. I have seen waves attack the wall like demons, recoiling and flinging themselves anew into the assault however often they were repulsed and broken into clouds of spray. One would think they must master the wall and bridge. Then the tide would assert itself and, in the fearfullest storm, make the waves recede. I was more aware of the rhythm of the tides at Portholland than anywhere else. The most deliberately dangerous thing I have ever done was to walk along the wall which separated the gardens of several cottages from the road across the beach, when the tide was high on one side and the gardens flooded on the other. I was dared to it. We—the village children of Caerhays and Portholland—were always daring each other. There were particular tests; bicycling down certain hills without brakes was included. We ought to have broken our necks.

Mrs. Johns's shop was on the right as we entered Portholland. We called it Mrs. Johns's for in it Mrs. Johns, or Carline as her husband, Tommy, called her, reigned supreme. Tommy had his boat, but Carline had the shop. When I knew her Mrs. Johns was already old, with beautiful silvery hair worn in a fashion all her own. It was parted in the middle, brought smoothly down over the ears, and fastened in a bunch of sausage curls at the back. I hardly remember seeing her out of doors; she was a stay-at-home. She once said to me when I offered her my piece of smoked glass to look at an eclipse of the sun, 'No, Anne, I do never like to gaze upon the heavenly bodies'. In the shop everything was sold from lard to lace. Biscuit tins fitted into their pigeon holes on the left, and at the back, facing the counter, were ranged the glass bottles of sweets which stuck together at times, and had to be stirred up with the yard measure before they could be induced to go into the little paper packets and be weighed up. We would scan the red and yellow pear-drops, the green translucent acid-drops, the pink and white peppermints, and the barcelona balls bulging with nuts, and falter in our choice. Chocolate was in wooden boxes; sheets of chocolate-coloured paper and crinkled pink paper were revealed when the lids were lifted. Fry's chocolate was the only kind, cakes of chocolate cream, or flat squares of plain chocolate. Mrs. Johns would say, 'Now which will 'ee have, clane or crame?'[1] Neat drawers which slid silkily in and out contained such things as currants and lemon peel, citron, tea, saffron, sultanas and rice. We envied Mrs. Johns these drawers. Nothing we could devise in playing shops could rival them, whereas the line for drapery on the right could easily be imitated. Red cotton handkerchiefs had pride of place on the line and, at Christmas-time, handkerchiefs having 'A Merry Christmas' worked in the corner in pink and blue, with a wonderful flourish issuing from the final S and rioting in prodigal amplitude about the whole design.

Tommy, sleeping partner to Carline in the shop, was master in his own boat. My brother Howard went out with him constantly when he was home for holidays, and I would go too. We took an oar each,

[1] Plain or cream.

and rowed for Tommy when he went out to see to his crab-pots. He would swear under his breath with an admirable diversity of expression at the spider crabs—damned old gavers. When we asked him questions as to the why or wherefore of the strange shapes and forms we peered down at in the clear deep water about the rocks, he would say 'I s'pose it was ordained so for to be'. His other reply was 'Aw, iss, iss'. We liked the early morning rows best of all. I still think the grey turning of waves on a beach just before dawn is the spectacle which catches one furthest away from those trivial occupations of living woven over and concealing the strangeness of being alive on the earth at all. One catches a glimpse of a world before time was and more lasting than life. The comfort and elation of sunrise after the greyness is expressed in 'O be joyful in the Lord, all ye lands'. My brother and I were silenced by the variety of sunrise from sullenness to splendour. Tommy's voice would be heard in the stillness, 'Pull right, pull left, pull left—aw my dear boys you've missed em both' as, sometimes mischievously, we made him miss the bobbing corks of the crab-pots. Tommy always included me in the masculine generic; he warned Howard against the girls. Once when he and Howard were looking over some nets together in the shed at West Portholland a number of girls drove down to bathe. Howard was watching them when Tommy said,

'Come in, my son, and veil yer eyes. They'm too many guns for you'.

The boat was kept at West Portholland where the cove was narrow and the sea deep in shore; there was no quay. The two coves were connected by a cliff road and, when the tide was out, by shoals of rocks at the cliff-foot, left bare and shining by the receding tide. To go from one Portholland to another, leaping at speed from rock to rock, was a sign that a boy or girl was no longer one of the little ones, but one of the big children. I completed this test almost immediately after my arrival in Caerhays, determined as I was to sustain the honour of Gorran in the eyes of new companions.

Perched on the cliff above West Portholland was the cottage of Miss Lucinda Hill. Blake's saying, 'Energy is eternal delight' was justified in her. She was always on the go with her tongue or her hand or her feet. She kept a cow, the pride of her eyes; a pig and fowls. To have a cow like Miss Hill's, and a boat like Tommy Johns's were my ambitions. Miss Hill's cow was no ordinary anonymous cow, but a personal friend, as indeed was the pig. A saying of Miss Hill's always remained with us. She often offered us a glass of skim-milk to drink after we had bathed, and she would say, 'Drink un up; pig don't want un'. Sometimes she gave us a bun which my brother did not like; he would hide his in his pocket while Lucinda was absent driving out the chickens who had a habit of intrusiveness. Once my brother forgot he had put his bun in his pocket and after Lucinda's return, in the course of conversation, he drew out his handkerchief and the bun with it. It fell on the floor in full sight, and for a moment we were speechlessly caught out. Then the one shining moment in my life of social aplomb occurred. 'He do keep his bun to eat going up Stony Hill', I said. 'Bless the chield', said Lucinda, 'eat un up; he shall have another to eat going up Stony Hill.' Crumb by crumb under Lucinda's gaze my brother ate his bun and was given another to put in his pocket to eat going up the Hill. Lucinda had a wonderful head of short grey curly hair, and her wrinkles were so deep and numerous as to be a glory. I can still hear her saying, 'Goodbye, my handsomes; and if mother do want a little chicken for Sunday, tell her I got a proper little one she can have'. She had a great fancy for my brother Howard. She would say to me when he was away, 'Bless his blue eyes. When is 'a coming home again?'

Susan never went to school at Caerhays. I had to face Caerhays children alone and felt very uneasy. It was not only a question of whether they would like me, but whether they would like my father. A schoolmaster's daughter can find life difficult. Naturally she is one with the children, but home affection butts in and prevents her from being happily agin the government when the popular tide is setting that way. Luckily for me relations between governor and governed were generally cordial both at Gorran and Caerhays. When they were not, with the fatal Cornish adaptability, I took the protective colour of my contemporaries. I came to love Caerhays school. It was a charming school, set back from the main road in a grass playground, and having great rounded windows to let in the sun, and open fireplaces to show the fire. The average attendance at the school ranged in my day from about twenty to thirty children. There were two rooms, a small room for the children under seven who were taught by a mistress, and the big room where all the other children were taught by my father. He had come to Caerhays because he had thought the work would be lighter. Actually he found it hard because of the age-range of the children. He worked out a scheme which was very like what is now known as the Dalton plan. Work was arranged for us and at certain times my father came round to the different groups to cope with difficulties. I certainly flourished under this method and liked it. For one thing I escaped the bugbear of reading aloud. For a quick, glancing, skimming reader this is always very tiresome, and detrimental. My father bought a large number of Stead's penny books—'Books for the Bairns'—and when we had finished the task in hand we could read to ourselves.

Also we could garden. The knowledge that there was something pleasant to do when we had finished a job encouraged us to work quickly. It is better to consider reading as a reward than as an examination subject.

I soon came to like Caerhays children, but I missed my Gorran friends and dearly liked to go back there. I used to say I was going over to have a little Gorran air. The air round Gorran really is different, more exhilarating and freer than the softer air of Caerhays. My father would often forget to post his weekly 'returns' to the District Clerk, and I would have an afternoon off sauntering over to Gorran to post them. Our post at Caerhays went out at eleven o'clock in the morning. Eleven o'clock at the pillar box by the Rectory gate, or else there was nothing for it but to go to Gorran. I did not mind how often the family forgot to post; I enjoyed the journey so much. I have discovered since that my father sometimes forgot on purpose to oblige me.

Caerhays was a church school built by Squire Williams, and maintained by him, until it was handed over to the Education Authority. My father had been promised complete freedom in the school; except for the rare and friendly visits of Inspectors, he obtained it. The Squire's attitude to the school was an amusing example of the very English habit of divergence between theory and practice. At Gorran the school was run by an education authority which was, in theory, committed heart and soul to the education of the people; in practice there was a certain niggardliness and cheese-paring; a neglect of warmth and sanitation.[1] At Caerhays I have heard my father say that theoretically the Squire was very cold towards bookish education, perhaps because, like us, he had known so many people of high integrity, good sense and religious feeling who had little of it. In theory he was less enthusiastic than a committee. In practice he provided a clean sunny school with blazing wood and coal fires in winter, and plenty of space everywhere. I think he never refused my father anything for the school from a field to a daffodil bulb.

Looking back it seems to me that the Squire's limitation was that he was rather a person who did his duty than one who enjoyed himself. He never sang in church. When he died bottles and bottles and bottles and bottles of wine had to have their necks broken and their lives lost because they had never been taken care of, much less drunk. I have been told that old Charlie H., who helped to cart the debris out to the Barns Hills, turned a somersault clean head-over-heels with his horse and his cart for joy of the mere smell of it. The Squire was incurably sober. He would give us a brace of pheasants but not the right bottle to go with them. Probably he

[1] But Mr. F. R. Pascoe, Secretary for Education, was an enthusiast. His delightfully vivid account of Cornish schools in the *Cornwall Education Week Handbook*, 1927, p. 37, is always worth re-reading.

would have been happier as a very private gentleman than as a man with great possessions which he felt he held as a trust. He was Lord Lieutenant of the Duchy, yet had no more taste for ceremony than for wine; he would rather look at a rhododendron bush than preside at a banquet. I can see him striding along on his great feet in big boots in a field ahead of us. He once stopped to spud up a thistle with his stick; it came up all of a sudden and over he went 'like a tab'. His word was law in Caerhays; perhaps that was why Gorran was different. There nobody's word was law however benevolent. 'I shall tell Ee about this', I can remember old Simon Rickard of the Lower Lodge saying to my father as he hobbled out rather late to open the gate for our pony-trap. Perhaps no human person should be Ee. Yet Ee kept his and our lovely Caerhays as lovely as when he inherited it. How else could it have been preserved from the jerry-builder and those who 'develop' Estates. Dodman Point, I think I am right in saying, was one of the very earliest of the National Trust properties. It was given by Squire Williams. To name the Trust in the same breath as the jerry-builders is wrong. Usually, I am glad to hear that places have come under the ownership of the Trust, and Ferguson's gang has seemed romantic to me. But I sometimes fear that even Cliffs will not bear embalming; and books like *Britain and the Beast: A Survey by Twenty-Six*

Authors[1] infuriate me because I hate sermons by people like Mr. C. E. M. Joad. He makes me feel contrary. If he inveighs against orange peel I want to flip a piece at him. He has all the new cant. The old cant of the Churches has been forgotten so long that all its phrases begin to wake up and take life again, fresh and endearing. But Mr. Joad uses, 'develop our latent potentialities'; 'newly enfranchised citizens of leisure' (this was before the war took away leisure from everybody); 'education in the appreciation of beauty'. He divides his sermon into three parts with sub-headings. Oh, oh, *oh*, Mr. Joad!

Squire Williams knew no cant. I have heard my father say no man was freer from the tyranny of words; I believe his advice was sought after in affairs. But I have never met people who were associated with him in public work. My memories of him are childish and with children he was probably at his best. He did not change his manner for them, but treated them with his accustomed gravity. If I met him out I knew he would shake hands with me as well as with my father, and that I should not have that awkward moment one had with most grown ups wondering whether one would shake hands or experience some equivalent to being patted on the head. Perhaps ceremony is freedom. I never remember his coming into school. Mrs. Williams

[1] Ed. Clough Williams Ellis, 1937.

came to give away the prizes. We had had no prizes at Gorran. On the whole I think it better for a school to be without prizes. Children are happy doing a thing for its own sake as long as no other motive is introduced. I sometimes think of Dr. Johnson's dictum when I consider the fiercely competitive nature of the system today: 'By exciting emulation and comparisons of superiority, you lay the foundations of lasting mischief; you make brothers and sisters hate each other.'

One thing prizes had encouraged at Caerhays was sewing. My eyes opened wide when I saw how the girls could sew. They were—the girls of my age and upwards—really beautiful needle-women. Their hands seemed cool and witty while mine were sticky and stupid. I can still see their clean cotton and delicate stitches contrasting with my dirty cotton, uneven tackings and drops of blood from my pricked fingers. The way they gathered and tucked and feather-stitched left me gaping with admiration. They cut just what was required whereas I, asked to snip an inch, would saw an ell. I never mastered the art of needlework.

It was after we had been at Caerhays three years or so that the question arose, 'What do you want to be?' I did not want to be anything. Susan seemed to be getting along quite nicely being nothing. But my parents said I must be something.

Unlike my sister I had no taste, apart from cooking, for domesticity. Even when I cooked I made more litter than a cook should and was inclined to shirk the saucepans. On one celebrated occasion I hid all the dirty dishes in the copper, a notion so entirely foreign to the tradition in which I had been brought up that I think I must have possessed original genius which failed to develop. I was always ready to flee the house. Like Mistress Anne Killigrew, whose poems I read in later years, I could have said:

> Arise, my Dove, from midst of Pots arise,
>   Thy sully'd habitation leave,
>   To dust no longer cleave,
> Unworthy they of Heaven that will not view
>   the skies.

There seemed nothing for it but for me to have a profession, for since I was not pretty I was not like to find an Earl of Leicester to install me in a bower of bliss above the pots and pans. If I did I might end down a trap-door.

My father was not anxious for me to teach. But what could I do? Nursing? I had a horror of it! Clerking? My figures would never add up! A shop-girl? I had a fancy I might like the grocery business, but Carline, when consulted by me, did not need a 'prentice. Somebody—a school-inspector, I think—said I had better try a Minor Scholarship for St. Austell. I was not displeased at this. It would not be as bad as a boarding school. I should have to live in St. Austell, but I should come home for week-ends. The idea of the examination did not worry me at all. My brothers had tossed off examination successes without losing any sleep, why should not I?

The day of trial drew near. I polished up Dart's hoofs for it and we drove in to St. Austell. I felt forlorn among the other candidates until I saw a girl with brown eyes and almost yellow curls. I conceived a romantic attachment to her on the spot, though I did not dream of speaking to her. She was laughing and careless and at ease. To my admiration she said in clear casual grown-up tones during the examination, 'May we have a window open, please?' May we have a window open, please! —with no shyness, just in ordinary tones. I hadn't even perceived what was wrong with the room, though I was stifling. As for boldly asking to have a window open, I should as soon have thought of playing bo-peep with the aged and bearded invigilator. I can remember only one question in the whole of the examination and that was 'Who wrote *Troy Town*?' I put an enormous Q, and informed my examiner that in my opinion *Dead Man's Rock* was the better book. By the time the examination was over I did not think I'd done so badly though my fingers were covered with ink, a good deal of which had conveyed itself in smears and smudges on the paper, and my handwriting looked no better than usual though I had taken pains. I did not wish to fail, though neither did I wish to go to St. Austell to school.

But I did fail. Some weeks afterwards I was sitting on the table in the kitchen shelling peas when my father came in and said, 'Well, Anne hasn't passed, so that's that!' My heart leapt up, although there was no rainbow in the sky. I said, 'So I shan't have to go to St. Austell, after all'. My father said, 'Not this year, any way'. Then he said, 'Mabel Teague has passed'. All my complacence slipped away. Mabel was my friend and contemporary at Gorran School, and I had thought we were about equal. My pride was distinctly hurt. I wished I had passed, even if it meant going away.

My family took my failure philosophically. My father laughed and said examiners threw all the papers against a sticky wall, and those that stuck passed, and those that dropped failed. I was never reproached. But I began to work at home. My father said I could try another scholarship, this time for intending teachers, next year; and that I'd better do some work so as not to be behind the others. We did together the first three books of Euclid and a good deal of Algebra; I began Latin, and I read as much history from as many different books as I could lay hold of. As a result, when I passed the examination a year later I was behind my contemporaries only in having no foreign languages. I remember nothing at all about the second examination.

The July and August before I went to St. Austell were halcyon days. I was free of one school and not in another. Howard was home for all August, and Maurice for part of it. Stan and Cap'n came for a fortnight in July. I drove up to meet them in turn at St. Austell and we came home to find the others watching for us by the gate below the church. This gate commanded a view of the road almost to Treberrick. It was a golden summer. Certain themes and airs of Chopin, Beethoven and Schubert bring it back with irresistible force. We were out all day and played and sang all the evening. I can hear Cap'n, a good baritone, singing 'Trumpeter, what are you sounding now?' with unconsciously prophetic feeling; or Maurice trolling out music-hall ditties; or Mr. Bellamy's one and only song, 'So we went strolling, over the rolling, over the rolling sea'. The hours seemed made for sunshine, or moonlight, or music, or making love. Everybody was falling in and out of love with the ease of early Shakespearean comedy. I remember the dust in the lanes through which the wheels of the trap went softly as I drove to St. Austell to meet this one or that; the clean leaves when the rain washed them; the swallows quartering the fields, skimming and turning with a speed that took one's breath away; the warm slow evening; the dumble dores blundering about with a scaly rattle. I would spend idle hours on the cliffs, watching grasshoppers like stiff-jointed bits of animated bracken, ladybirds with varnished spotted cases into which to fold their gauze wings. 'Ladybird, ladybird, fly away home.' I used to wish I could be compact and complete like the ladybird, secure against the weather, yet unburdened; able to fly.

There was one excursion we always made when one or two of my brothers and their friends or current lady-loves were at home. We would have Johnny Johns's wagonette, and get up very early in the morning, and drive first to Portscatho, then on to Percuil where we got a steamer. We went by steamer to Falmouth where we stayed an hour or so, then we boarded *The Queen of the Fal* for the trip to Truro and back.

I did not care particularly for Falmouth in those days. But some years after, when I was camping at St. Antony in Roseland, I bicycled in the cool of the evening to the Lighthouse by Zoze Point, and realized for the first time in my life the splendour of Falmouth harbour. In my arrogance I had thought of Falmouth (God forgive me) as a place for 'visitors' and to be avoided. But when towards sunset I stood on the rocks below the lighthouse, facing the harbour, I knew that everything that had ever been written or said about the beauty of Falmouth harbour was true. The sun made a broad road of gold between me and the Castle; crossing this road the sails of the boats turned gold. The sea was merry with a gently-ruffling breeze. The estuary had an aspect of glorious spaciousness; and from it the tide ran up into land, up the creeky Fal, running up to Penryn, running up to Malpas and Truro, running up to Percuil; it used ages ago even to run up to Tregony. Facing me the outline of the Promontory was sharp and clear with the sun at its back hiding Falmouth town. The docks lay to the right with big ships hinting of the busy sea-traffic of bygone Falmouth. I watched the hills at the back and the far-distant smooth lines of a carn. To the left the coast stretched in a long line in shadow to the Manacles. I saw the sun set, and at the moment of its setting the lighthouse light—and I suppose all other lighthouse lights in Cornwall—came on. No wonder that to the Cornish the lighthouse lights seem as punctual and natural as the heavenly bodies. I have always liked the late Charles Henderson's story of the old man at the Lizard who wanted the parson to read him a passage from the Bible and asked for the passage about Lizard Lights. The parson was puzzled till it was explained to him that the passage was 'The sun, the moon and all the lesser (Lezzard) lights'.

In the old days of our visits to Falmouth I cared more for Jacob's Ladder than the Lighthouse or the Castle, though the harbour was always a source of pleasure and anxiety. People would be grumbling

at the iniquity of having to give a penny to go through
the turnstile on to Princes Pier; and once on the
pier the crowd seeking *The Queen of the Fal* would
surge towards a set of steps. After we had been
there some time an old man in a peaked cap would
shout with malicious joy, 'This way for *The Queen
of the Fal*', and the crowd would surge in his direction, the last persons now becoming first, and all
elbowing and jostling till one was nearly shoved
into the water. It seemed as though there would
never be room for us all; but soon the last person
was handed aboard and there we were, up-country
people, and Cornish folk, and haughty persons in
full yachtsman's rig, looking so much more nautical
than any *nauta* I have ever seen.

A churning and a hooting, and we would move
off through the dancing water of the bay into the
smooth heavy river water, the scene ever shifting and
changing as we advanced; the prospect now opening
up, now closing in on us, till it seemed we were
land-locked and could progress no further; then
we would round a bend into fresh reaches, with
banks wooded to the water's edge, dwarf oak and
rose and thorn. I used to think I would like to live
at Pill Creek; or one could perhaps become ferryman at King Harry Passage, with the ferryman's
money to live on and a little house thrown in. There
are dear little houses on the banks of the Fal.

And so we would come to Malpas and to Truro

217

which looks its best from the river, once you have passed municipal ugliness and come to the wharfs. The Cathedral was the first Protestant Cathedral, with the exception of St. Paul's, to be built in England after the Reformation. The site is the old St. Mary's Church; and as that in its turn stood in the old High Cross, the place has had Christian associations for many centuries, though it is only just over fifty years ago that the choir and part of the nave of the Cathedral were consecrated, and the lovely Western towers were not finished until 1910. Those learned in cathedral architecture have always found it difficult to judge Truro Cathedral for what it is in itself. Knowing that it is imitation Early English, they have looked at it and, expecting it to be lifeless, have found it so. They have not seen its freshness nor its suitability for Truro as Truro is—the market city, not of the wilder parts of Cornwall, but of the tilled and cultivated Roseland district, a land of little woods and cornfields, a southern and sunny place. To appreciate Truro Cathedral one must come towards it in *The Queen of the Fal* past the sheltered creeks and orchards. Then the spires are necessary and right.

Mabe granite went to the making of the outside of Truro Cathedral and, although much Bath stone is used inside, china-claystone from St. Stephen's has its place, grey polyphant from east Cornwall, and Lizard serpentine. The clock tower is roofed

with Cornish copper, and the colour adds a note of
fantasy, as though some jinnee with a sense of the
ridiculous had come and clapped this green cap on
in the night while the builders slept . . .

I was confirmed in the Cathedral the summer of
the year I passed the scholarship examination. Alas,
just as Karen thought of her red shoes, I thought
of my new white frock.

I tried to make time go slowly that summer,
and enjoyed everything with the sharpened pleasure
of one about to go into captivity. Lodgings had
been found for me at St. Austell in a little crooked
house full of cats. Grant's Walk was the alley, and
through it in addition to the cats of my hostess,
Miss Susan V—, walked all the cats of St. Austell,
black and tabby, white and marmalade, short-
tailed and long. The alley was jewelled with eyes.
I was not anxious about my lodgings. I knew I
should like them; but about the school I was filled
with anxiety. How should I fare among all these
youths and maidens and what should I do without the
sea and Dart? I began to pity myself; I envied Susan.

My mother talked of clothes. The only clothes
I had were made up of such odd bits of bright
coloured stuff as had come my mother's way from
various aunts. I loved bright colours. But my
aunt assured my mother that a navy blue suit was
what I needed, and though my mother said doubt-
fully she'd never fancied me in navy blue my

worldly-wise aunt's advice prevailed. Navy blue it was; and when it came fresh from a Truro tailor's I put it on and felt like a snuffed candle. I suppose I had other clothes; but in that navy blue I changed from being a poppy into something sober like pennywort. I wished with all my heart I'd had the sense to fail the examination a second time.

Term began on a Tuesday. On the Saturday I drove my own luggage in to Grant's Walk, pretending to myself in the gloomiest fashion that the trunk was my coffin. I told Dart I should die young; and at Faircross I nearly ran into Mr. Bellamy's dog-cart while shedding imaginary tears at my own funeral. Mr. Bellamy was returning from Grampound. He stopped and cheered me up and, if it hadn't been awkward with the two ponies and traps, would have turned back and accompanied me into St. Austell himself to console me with tea and buns. As it was we agreed it wouldn't be very companionable to drive six miles together in separate traps, so he went off home to his nice Rectory. I've had a hankering to be ordained ever since, and a fancy for the title of Rural Dean.

At first it was said that my father would drive me in for the first school day on Monday evening so that I should be all shining and ready for Tuesday morning. But I pleaded so hard to stay until Tuesday morning that my parents allowed it. It meant my mother's driving me in, and she hated the lonely roads. However, she did it. We started at about 7.30 and she drove me as far as St. Mewan from which I was to walk. I tried to drive slowly but Dart was lively, tossing his head, and full of early morning tricks. We reached St. Mewan hill in no time. I turned the trap for my mother, kissed her and kissed Dart. He took no notice. He was too full of joy at being turned for home at St. Mewan instead of having to go in to St. Austell. He frisked off in high spirits, and soon he and the trap and my mother in her old brown golf cape with its plaid hood were lost to view. I knew I should be late. I walked slowly to make myself later. I meditated on schemes by which I might take to the woods from Monday to Friday nights, and yet make it appear to my parents that I had been to school all the time. If only I could become a Palmer or a Gaberlunzie. Slower and slower I walked, but at last I came to the door of the disused chapel in which the school was being held while its new quarters were a-building. I opened the door and went in.

THE CORNISH LIBRARY

Cornwall has a literary heritage quite out of proportion to its geographical size. Since Richard Carew of Antony first published his *Survey of Cornwall* in 1602 its native writers have consistently produced outstanding works of history, biography, poetry, and fiction. At the same time the Cornish landscape and the peculiar character of the Celtic peninsula – part English county, part independent nation – have inspired visiting writers to works of extraordinary power and imagination.

The Cornish Library is a new publishing venture, dedicated to presenting in attractive, paperback editions some of the best and most lasting books on Cornwall and the Cornish, both fiction and non-fiction. And because this phenomenon of Cornish literature is not simply a proud inheritance but a living potential *The Cornish Library* will, as it develops, include original works on a wide range of subjects.

The first titles to appear in *The Cornish Library* are as follows:

1. Up From The Lizard   *J. C. Trewin*
2. A Cornish Childhood   *A. L. Rowse*
3. Freedom of the Parish   *Geoffrey Grigson*
4. School House in the Wind   *Anne Treneer*

In preparation are works by Wilkie Collins, Thomas Hardy, Q, Crosbie Garstin, Bernard Walke, and Compton Mackenzie. Entirely new titles will include *A Short History of Cornwall*, *Cornish Country Houses and Gardens*, and *Wild Flowers of Cornwall*.

All the books in *The Cornish Library* will be numbered to encourage collectors. If you would like more information, or you would care to suggest books that you think should appear in the series, please write to me at the following address:

Anthony Mott
The Cornish Library
50 Stile Hall Gardens
London W4 3BU